Tanglewood Tales

Nathaniel Hawthorne

Sharon Publications, Inc.
Closter, NJ

CONTENTS

The Wayside—Introductory

A SHORT time ago, I was favored with a flying visit from my young friend Eustace Bright, whom I had not before met with since quitting the breezy mountains of Berkshire. It being the winter vacation at his college, Eustace was allowing himself a little relaxation, in the hope, he told me, of repairing the inroads which severe application to study had made upon his health; and I was happy to conclude, from the excellent physical condition in which I saw him, that the remedy had already been attended with very desirable success. He had now run up from Boston by the noon train, partly impelled by the friendly regard with which he is pleased to honor me, and partly, as I soon found, on a matter of literary business.

It delighted me to receive Mr. Bright, for the first time, under a roof, though a very humble one, which I could really call my own. Nor did I fail (as is the custom of landed proprietors all about the world) to parade the poor fellow up and down over my half a dozen acres; secretly rejoicing, nevertheless, that the disarray of the inclement season, and particularly the six inches of snow then upon the ground, prevented him from observing the ragged neglect of soil and shrubbery into which the place had lapsed. It was idle, however, to imagine that an airy guest from Monument Mountain, Bald Summit, and old Greylock, shaggy with primeval forests, could see anything to admire in my poor little hillside, with its growth of frail and insect-eaten locust trees. Eustace very frankly called the view from my hilltop tame; and so, no doubt, it was, after rough, broken, rugged, headlong Berkshire, and especially the northern parts of the country with which his college residence had made him familiar. But to me there is a peculiar, quiet charm in these broad meadows and gentle eminences. They are better than mountains, because they do not stamp and stereotype themselves into the brain, and thus grow wearisome with the same strong impression repeated day after day. A few summer weeks among mountains, a lifetime among green meadows and placid slopes, with outlines forever new, because continually fading out of the memory — such would be my sober choice.

I doubt whether Eustace did not internally pronounce the whole thing a bore, until I led him to my predecessor's little ruined, rustic summerhouse, midway on the hillside. It is a mere skeleton of slender, decaying tree trunks, with neither walls nor a roof; nothing but a tracery of branches and twigs, which the next winter blast will be very likely to scatter in fragments along the terrace. It looks, and is, as evanescent as a dream; and yet, in its rustic network of boughs, it has somehow inclosed a hint of spiritual beauty, and has become a true emblem of the subtile and ethereal mind that planned it. I made Eustace Bright sit down on a snow bank, which had heaped itself over the mossy seat, and gazing through the arched window opposite, he acknowledged that the scene at once grew picturesque.

"Simple as it looks," said he, "this little edifice seems to be the work of magic. It is full of suggestiveness, and, in its way, is as good as a cathedral. Ah, it would be just the spot for one to sit in, of a summer afternoon, and tell the children some more of those wild stories from the classic myths!"

"It would, indeed," answered I. "The summer-house itself, so airy and so broken, is like one of those old tales, imperfectly remembered; and these living branches of the Baldwin apple tree, thrusting themselves so rudely in, are like your unwarrantable interpolations. But, by the by, have you added any more legends to the series, since the publication of the Wonder Book?"

"Many more," said Eustace; "Primrose, Periwinkle, and the rest of them allow me no comfort of my life, unless I tell them a story every day or two. I have written out six of the new stories, and have brought them for you to look over."

"Are they as good as the first?" I inquired.

"Better chosen and better handled," replied Eustace Bright. "You will say so when you read them."

"Possibly not," I remarked. "I know, from my own experience, that an author's last work is always his best one, in his own estimate, until it quite loses the red heat of composition. After that, it falls into its true place quietly enough.

But let us adjourn to my study, and examine these new stories. It would hardly be doing yourself justice, were you to bring me acquainted with them, sitting here on this snow bank!"

So we descended the hill to my small, old cottage, and shut ourselves up in the southeastern room, where the sunshine comes in warmly and brightly through the better half of a winter's day. Eustace put his bundle of manuscript into my hands; and I skimmed through it pretty rapidly, trying to find out its merits and demerits by the touch of my fingers, as a veteran story-teller ought to know how to do.

It will be remembered that Mr. Bright condescended to avail himself of my literary experience by constituting me editor of the Wonder Book. As he had no reason to complain of the reception of that erudite work by the public, he was now disposed to retain me in a similar position, with respect to the present volume, which he entitled Tanglewood Tales. Not, as Eustace hinted, that there was any real necessity for my services as introductor, inasmuch as his own name had become established, in some good degree of favor, with the literary world. But the connection with myself, he was kind enough to say, had been highly agreeable; nor was he by any means desirous, as most people are, of kicking away the ladder that had perhaps helped him to reach his present elevation. My young friend was willing, in short, that the fresh verdure of his growing reputation should spread over my straggling and half-naked boughs; even as I have sometimes thought of training a vine, with its broad leafiness, and purple fruitage, over the worm-eaten posts and rafters of the rustic summerhouse. I was not insensible to the advantages of his proposal, and gladly assured him of my acceptance.

Merely from the titles of the stories, I saw at once that the subjects were not less rich than those of the former volume; not did I at all doubt that Mr. Bright's audacity (so far as that endowment might avail) had enabled him to take full advantage of whatever capabilities they offered. Yet, in spite of my experience of his free way of handling them, I did not quite see, I confess, how he could have obviated all the difficulties in the way of rendering them presentable to children. These old legends, so brimming over with everything that is most abhorrent to our Christianized moral sense — some of them so hideous, others so melancholy and miserable, amid which the Greek tragedians sought their themes, and molded them into the sternest forms of grief that ever the world saw; was such material the stuff that children's playthings should be made of! How were they to be purified? How was the blessed sunshine to be thrown into them?

But Eustace told me that these myths were the most singular things in the world, and that he was invariably astonished, whenever he began to relate one, by the readiness with which it adapted itself to the childish purity of his auditors. The objectionable characteristics seem to be a parasitical growth, having no essential connection with the original fable. They fall away, and are thought of no more, the instant he puts his imagination in sympathy with the innocent little circle, whose wide-open eyes are fixed so eagerly upon him. Thus the stories (not by any strained effort of the narrator's, but in harmony with their inherent germ) transform themselves, and reassume the shapes which they might be supposed to possess in the pure childhood of the world. When the first poet or romancer told these marvelous legends (such is Eustace Bright's opinion), it was still the Golden Age. Evil had never yet existed; and sorrow, misfortune, crime, were mere shadows which the mind fancifully created for itself, as a shelter against too sunny realities; or, at most, but prophetic dreams, to which the dreamer himself did not yield a waking credence. Children are now the only representatives of the men and women of that happy year; and therefore it is that we must raise the intellect and fancy to the level of childhood, in order to recreate the original myths.

I let the youthful author talk as much and as extravagantly as he pleased, and was glad to see him commencing life with such confidence in himself and his performances. A few years will do all that is necessary toward showing him the truth in both respects. Meanwhile, it is but right to say, he does really appear to have overcome the moral objections against these fables, although at the expense of such liberties with their structure as must be left to plead their own excuse, without any help from me. Indeed, except that there was a necessity for it — and that the inner life of the legends cannot be come at save by making them entirely one's own property — there is no defense to be made.

Eustace informed me that he had told his stories to the children in various situations — in the woods, on the shore of the lake, in the dell of Shadow Brook, in the play room, at Tanglewood fireside, and in a magnificent palace of snow, with ice windows, which he helped his little friends to build. His auditors were even more delighted with the contents of the present volume than with the specimens which have already been given to the world. The classically learned Mr. Pringle, too, had listened to two or three of the tales, and censured them even more bitterly than he did "The Three Golden Apples"; so that, what with praise, and what with criticism, Eustace Bright thinks that there is good hope of at least as much success with the public as in the case of the Wonder Book.

I made all sorts of inquiries about the children, not doubting that there would be great eagerness to hear of their welfare, among some good little folks who have written to me, to ask for another volume of myths. They are all, I am happy to say (unless we except Clover), in excellent health and spirits. Primrose is now almost a young lady, and, Eustace tells me, is just as saucy as ever. She pretends to consider herself quite beyond the age to be interested by such idle stories as these; but, for all that, whenever a story is to be told, Primrose never fails to be one of the listeners, and to make fun of it when finished. Periwinkle is very much grown, and is expected to shut up her baby house and throw away her doll in a month or two more. Sweet Fern has learned to read and write, and has put on a jacket and a pair of pantaloons — all of which improvements I am sorry for. Squash Blossom, Blue Eye, Plantain, and Buttercup have had the scarlet fever, but came easily through it. Huckleberry, Milkweed, and Dandelion were attacked with the whooping cough, but bore it bravely, and kept out of doors whenever the sun shone. Cowslip, during the autumn, had either the measles, or some eruption that looked very much like it, but was hardly sick a day. Poor Clover has been a good deal troubled with her second teeth, which have made her meager in aspect and rather fractious in temper; nor, even when she smiles, is the matter much mended, since it discloses a gap just within her lips, almost as wide as the barn door. But all this will pass over, and it is predicted that she will turn out a very pretty girl.

As for Mr. Bright himself, he is now in his senior year at Williams College, and has a prospect of graduating with some degree of honorable distinction at the next commencement. In his oration for the bachelor's degree, he gives me to understand he will treat one of the classical myths viewed in the aspect of baby's stories, and has a great mind to discuss the expediency of using up the whole of ancient history, for the same purpose. I do not know what he means to do with himself after leaving college, but trust that, by dabbling so early with the dangerous and seductive business of authorship, he will not be tempted to become an author by profession. If so, I shall be very sorry for the little that I have had to do with the matter, in encouraging these first beginnings.

I wish there were any likelihood of my soon seeing Primrose, Periwinkle, Dandelion, Sweet Fern, Clover, Plantain, Huckleberry, Milkweed, Cowslip, Buttercup, Blue Eye, and Squash Blossom again. But as I do not know when I shall revisit Tanglewood, and as Eustace Bright probably will not ask me to edit a third Wonder Book, the public of little folks must not expect to hear any more about those dear children from me.   Heaven bless them, and everybody else, whether grown people or children!

The Minotaur

IN the old city of Trœzene, at the foot of a lofty mountain, there lived, a very long time ago, a little boy named Theseus. His grandfather, King Pittheus, was the sovereign of that country, and was reckoned a very wise man; so that Theseus, being brought up in the royal palace, and being naturally a bright lad, could hardly fail of profiting by the old king's instructions. His mother's name was Æthra. As for his father, the boy had never seen him. But, from his earliest remembrance, Æthra used to go with little Theseus into a wood, and sit down upon a mossgrown rock, which was deeply sunken into the earth. Here she often talked with her son about his father, and said that he was called Ægeus, and that he was a great king, and ruled over Attica, and dwelt at Athens, which was as famous a city as any in the world. Theseus was very fond of hearing about King Ægeus, and often asked his good mother Æthra why he did not come and live with them at Trœzene.

"Ah, my dear son," answered Æthra, with a sigh, "a monarch has his people to take care of.

The men and women over whom he rules are in the place of children to him; and he can seldom spare time to love his own children as other parents do. Your father will never be able to leave his kingdom for the sake of seeing his little boy."

"Well, but, dear mother," asked the boy, "why cannot I go to this famous city of Athens and tell King Ægeus that I am his son?"

"That may happen by and by," said Æthra. "Be patient, and we shall see. You are not yet big and strong enough to set out on such an errand."

"And how soon shall I be strong enough?" Theseus persisted in inquiring.

"You are but a tiny boy as yet," replied his mother. "See if you can lift this rock on which we are sitting."

The little fellow had a great opinion of his own strength. So, grasping the rough protuberances of the rock he tugged and toiled amain, and got himself quite out of breath, without being able to stir the heavy stone. It seemed to be rooted into the ground. No wonder he could not move it; for it would have taken all the force of a very strong man to lift it out of its earthy bed.

His mother stood on, with a sad kind of smile on her lips and in her eyes, to see the zealous and yet puny efforts of her little boy. She could not help being sorrowful at finding him already so impatient to begin his adventures in the world.

"You see how it is, my dear Theseus," said she. "You must possess far more strength thán now before I can trust you to go to Athens, and tell King Ægeus that you are his son. But when you can lift this rock, and show me what is hidden beneath it, I promise you my permission to depart."

Often and often, after this, did Theseus ask his mother whether it was yet time for him to go to Athens; and still his mother pointed to the rock, and told him that, for years to come, he could not be strong enough to move it. And again and again the rosy-cheeked and curly-headed boy would tug and strain at the huge mass of stone, striving, child as he was, to do what a giant could hardly have done without taking both of his great hands to the task. Meanwhile the rock seemed to be sinking farther and farther into the ground. The moss grew over it thicker and thicker, until at last it looked almost like a soft green seat, with only a few gray knobs of granite peeping out. The over-hanging trees, also, shed their brown leaves upon it, as often as the autumn came; and at its base grew ferns and wild flowers, some of which crept quite over its surface. To all appearance, the rock was as firmly fastened as any other portion of the earth's substance.

But, difficult as the matter looked, Theseus was not growing up to be such a vigorous youth, that, in his own opinion, the time would quickly come when he might hope to get the upper hand of this ponderous lump of stone.

"Mother, I do believe that it has started!" cried he, after one of his attempts. "The earth around it has certainly cracked!"

"No, no, child!" his mother hastily answered. "It is not possible that you can have moved it, such a boy as you still are!"

Nor would she be convinced, although Theseus showed her the place where he fancied that the stem of a flower had been partly uprooted by the movement of the rock. But AEthra sighed and looked disquieted; for, no doubt, she began to be conscious that her son was no longer a child, and that, in a little while hence, she must send him forth among the perils and troubles of the world.

It was not more than a year afterwards when they were again sitting on the moss-covered stone. AEthra had once more told him the oft-repeated story of his father, and how gladly he would receive Theseus at his stately palace, and how he would present him to his courtiers and the people, and tell them that here was the heir of his dominions. The eyes of Theseus glowed with enthusiasm, and he would hardly sit still to hear his mother speak.

"Dear mother AEthra," he exclaimed, "I never felt half so strong as now! I am no longer a child nor a boy nor a mere youth! I feel myself a man! It is now time to make one earnest trial to remove the stone."

"Ah, my dearest Theseus," replied his mother, "not yet! not yet!"

"Yes, mother," said he, resolutely, "the time has come!"

Then Theseus bent himself in good earnest to the task, and strained every sinew, with manly strength and resolution. He put his whole brave heart into the effort. He wrestled with the big and sluggish stone, as if it had been a living enemy. He heaved, he lifted, he resolved now to succeed, or else to perish there, and let the rock be his monument forever! AEthra stood gazing at him, and clasped her hands, partly with a mother's pride, and partly with a mother's sorrow. The great rock stirred! Yes, it was raised slowly from the bedded moss and earth, uprooting the shrubs and flowers along with it, and was turned upon its side. Theseus had conquered!

While taking breath, he looked joyfully at his mother, and she smiled upon him through her tears.

"Yes, Theseus," she said, "the time has come, and you must stay no longer at my side! See what King AEgeus, your royal father, left for you, beneath the stone, when he lifted it in his mighty arms, and laid it on the spot whence you have now removed it."

Theseus looked, and saw that the rock had been placed over another slab of stone, containing a cavity within it; so that it somewhat resembled a roughly made chest or coffer, of which the upper mass had served as the lid. Within the cavity lay a sword, with a golden hilt, and a pair of sandals.

"That was your father's sword," said AEthra, "and those were his sandals. When he went to be king of Athens, he bade me treat you as a child until you should prove yourself a man by lifting this heavy stone. That task being accomplished, you are to put on his sandals, in order to follow in your father's footsteps, and to gird on his sword, so that you may fight giants and dragons, as King AEgeus did in his youth."

"I will set out for Athens this very day!" cried Theseus.

But his mother persuaded him to stay a day or two longer, while she got ready some necessary articles for his journey. When his grandfather, the wise King Pittheus, heard that Theseus intended to present himself at his father's

palace, he earnestly advised him to get on board
a vessel and go by sea; because he might thus
arrive within fifteen miles of Athens, without
either fatigue or danger.

"The roads are very bad by land," quoth the
venerable king; "and they are terribly infested
with robbers and monsters. A mere lad, like
Theseus, is not fit to be trusted on such a
perilous journey, all by himself. No, no; let him
go by sea!"

But when Theseus heard of robbers and monsters, he pricked up his ears, and was so much
more the more eager to take the road along
which they were to be met with. On the third
day, therefore, he bade a respectful farewell to
his grandfather, thanking him for all his kindness;
and, after affectionately embracing his mother,
he set forth, with a good many of her tears
glistening on his cheeks, and some, if the truth
must be told, that had gushed out of his own
eyes. But he let the sun and wind dry them, and
walked stoutly on, playing with the golden hilt of
his sword, and taking very manly strides in his
father's sandals.

I cannot stop to tell you hardly any of the
adventures that befell Theseus on the road to
Athens. It is enough to say that he quite cleared
that part of the country of the robbers, about
whom King Pittheus had been so much alarmed.
One of these bad people was named Procrustes;
and he was indeed a terrible fellow, and had an
ugly way of making fun of the poor travelers who
happened to fall into his clutches. In his cavern
he had a bed, on which, with great pretense of
hospitality, he invited his guests to lie down; but
if they happened to be shorter than the bed, this

wicked villain stretched them out by main force;
or, if they were too tall, he lopped off their
heads or feet, and laughed at what he had done,
as an excellent joke. Thus, however weary a man
might be, he never liked to lie in the bed of
Procrustes. Another of these robbers, named
Scinis, must have likewise have been a very great
scoundrel. He was in the habit of flinging his
victims off a high cliff into the sea; and, in order
to give him exactly his deserts, Theseus tossed
him off the very same place. But if you will
believe me, the sea would not pollute itself by
receiving such a bad person into its bosom,
neither would the earth, having once got rid of
him, consent to take him back; so that, between
the cliff and the sea, Scinis stuck fast in the air,
which was forced to bear the burden of his
naughtiness.

After these memorable deeds, Theseus heard
of an enoumous sow which ran wild, and was the
terror of all the farmers round about; and, as he
did not consider himself above doing any good
thing that came in his way, he killed this
monstrous creature, and gave the carcass to the
poor people for bacon. The great sow had been
an awful beast, while ramping about the woods
and fields, but was a pleasant object enough
when cut up into joints, and smoking on I know
not how many dinner tables.

Thus, by the time he reached his journey's end,
Theseus had done many valiant feats with his
father's golden-hilted sword, and had gained the
renown of being one of the bravest young men of
the day. His fame traveled faster than he did,
and reached Athens before him. As he entered
the city, he heard the inhabitants talking at the

street corners and saying that Hercules was brave, and Jason too, and Castor and Pollux likewise, but that Theseus, the son of their own king, would turn out as great a hero as the best of them. Theseus took longer strides on hearing this, and fancied himself sure of a magnificent reception at his father's court, since he came thither with Fame to blow her trumpet before him, and cry to King Ægeus, "Behold! your son!"

He little suspected, innocent youth that he was, that here in this very Athens, where his father reigned, a greater danger awaited him than any which he had encountered on the road. Yet this was the truth. You must understand that the father of Theseus, though not very old in years, was almost worn out with the cares of government, and had thus grown aged before his time. His nephews, not expecting him to live a very great while, intended to get all the power of the kingdom into their own hands. But when they heard that Theseus had arrived in Athens, and learned what a gallant young man he was, they saw that he would not be at all the kind of person to let them steal away his father's crown and sceptor, which ought to be his own by right of inheritance. Thus these bad-hearted nephews of King Ægeus, who were the own cousins of Theseus, at once became his enemies. A still more dangerous enemy was Medea, the wicked enchantress; for she was now the king's wife, and wanted to give the kingdom to her son Medus, instead of letting it be given to the son of Æthra, whom she hated.

It so happened that the king's nephews met Theseus, and found out who he was, just as he reached the entrance of the royal palace. With all their evil designs against him, they pretended to be their cousin's best friends, and expressed great joy at making his acquaintance. They proposed to him that he should come into the king's presence as a stranger, in order to try whether AEgeus would discover in the young man's features any likeness wither to himself or his mother AEthra, and thus recognize him for a son. Theseus consented; for he fancied that his father would know him in a moment, by the love that was in his heart. But, while he waited at the door, the nephews ran and told King AEgeus that a young man had arrived in Athens, who, to their certain knowledge, intended to put him to death, and get possession of his royal crown.

"And he is now waiting for admission to your Majesty's presence," added they.

"Aha!" cried the old king, on hearing this. "Why, he must be a very wicked young fellow indeed! Pray, what would you advise me to do with him!"

In reply to this question, the wicked Medea put in her word. As I have already told you, she was a famous enchantress. According to some stories, she was in the habit of boiling old people in a large caldron, under pretense of making them young again; but King AEgeus, I suppose, did not fancy such an uncomfortable way of growing young, or perhaps was contented to be old, and therefore would never let himself be popped into the caldron. If there were time to spare from more important matters, I should be glad to tell you of Medea's fiery chariot, drawn by winged dragons, in which the enchantress used often to take an airing among the clouds. This chariot, in fact, was the vehicle that first brought her to Athens, where she had done nothing but mischief ever since her arrival. But these and many other wonders must be left untold; and it is enough to say that Medea, amongst a thousand other bad things, knew how to prepare a poison that was instantly fatal to whomsoever might so much as touch it with his lips.

So when the king asked what he should do with Theseus, this naughty woman had an answer ready at her tongue's end.

"Leave that to me, please your Majesty," she replied. "Only admit this evil-minded young man to your presence, treat him civilly, and invite him to drink a goblet of wine. Your Majesty is well aware that I sometimes amuse myself with distilling very powerful medicines. Here is one of them in this small phial. As to what it is made of, that is one of my secrets of state. Do but let me put a single drop into the goblet, and let the young man taste it; and I will answer for it, he shall quite lay aside the bad designs with which he comes hither."

As she said this, Medea smiled; but, for all her smiling face, she meant nothing less than to poison the poor innocent Theseus, before his father's eyes. And King AEgeus, like most other kings, thought any punishment mild enough, for a person who was accused of plotting against his life. He therefore made little or no objection to Medea's scheme, and as soon as the poisonous wine was ready, gave orders that the young stranger should be admitted into his presence. The goblet was set on a table beside the king's throne; and a fly, meaning just to sip a little from the brim, immediately tumbled into it, dead.   Observing this, Medea looked around at the nephews, and smiled again.

When Theseus was ushered into the royal apartment, the only object that he seemed to behold was the white-bearded old king. There he sat on his magnificent throne, a dazzling crown on his head, and a scepter in his hand. His aspect was stately and majestic, although his years and infirmities weighed heavily upon him, as if each year were a lump of lead, and each infirmity a ponderous stone, and all were bundled up together, and laid upon his weary shoulders. The tears both of joy and sorrow sprang into the young man's eyes; for he thought how sad it was to see his dear father so infirm, and how sweet it would be to support him with his own youthful strength, and to cheer him up with the alacrity of his loving spirit. When a son takes his father into his warm heart, it renews the old man's youth in a better way than by the heat of Medea's magic caldron. And this was what Theseus resolved to do. He could scarcely wait to see whether King Ægeus would recognize him, so eager was he to throw himself into his arms.

Advancing to the foot of the throne, he attempted to make a little speech, which he had been thinking about, as he came up the stairs. But he was almost choked by a great many tender feelings that gushed out of his heart and swelled into his throat, all struggling to find utterance together. And therefore, unless he could have laid his full, overbrimming heart into the king's hand, poor Theseus knew not what to do or say. The cunning Medea observed what was passing in the young man's mind. She was more wicked at that moment than ever she had been before; for (and it makes me tremble to tell you of it) she did her worst to turn all this unspeakable love with which Theseus was agitated, to his own ruin and destruction.

"Does your Majesty see his confusion?" she whispered in the king's ear. "He is so conscious of guilt that he trembles and cannot speak. The wretch lives too long! Quick! offer him the wine!"

Now King Ægeus had been gazing earnestly at the young stranger, as he drew near the throne. There was something, he knew not what, either in his white brow, or in the fine expression of his mouth, or in his beautiful and tender eyes, that made him indistinctly feel as if he had seen this youth before; as if, indeed, he had trotted him on his knee when a baby, and had beheld him growing to be a stalwart man, while he himself grew old. But Medea guessed how the king felt, and would not suffer him to yield to these natural sensibilities; although they were the voice of his deepest heart, telling him, as plainly as it could speak, that here was his dear son, and Æthra's son, coming to claim him for a father. The enchantress again whispered in the king's ear, and compelled him, by her witchcraft, to see everything under a false aspect.

He made up his mind, therefore, to let Theseus drink off the poisoned wine.

"Young man," said he, "you are welcome! I am proud to show hospitality to so heroic a youth. Do me the favor to drink the contents of this goblet. It is brimming over, as you see, with delicious wine, such as I bestow only on those who are worthy of it! None is more worthy to quaff it than yourself!"

So saying, King Ægeus took the golden goblet
from the table, and was about to offer it to
Theseus. But, partly through his infirmities, and
partly because it seemed so sad a thing to take
away this young man's life, however wicked he
might be, and partly, no doubt, because his heart
was wiser than his head, and quaked within him
at the thought of what he was going to do — for
all these reasons, the king's hand trembled so
much that a great deal of the wine slopped over.
In order to strengthen his purpose, and fearing
lest the whole of the precious poison should be
wasted, one of his nephews now whispered to
him:

"Has your Majesty any doubt of his stranger's
guilt? There is the very sword with which he
meant to slay you. How sharp and bright and
terrible it is! Quick! — let him taste the wine;
or perhaps he may do the deed even yet."

At these words, Ægeus drove every thought
and feeling out of his breast, except the one idea
of how justly the young man deserved to be put
to death. He sat erect on his throne, and held
out the goblet of wine with a steady hand, and
bent on Theseus a frown of kingly severity; for,
after all, he had too noble a spirit to murder
even a treacherous enemy with a deceitful smile
upon his face.

"Drink!" said he, in the stern tone with which
he was wont to condemn a criminal to be
beheaded. "You have well deserved of me such
wine as this!"

Theseus held out his hand to take the wine.
But, before he touched it, King Ægeus trembled
again. His eyes had fallen on the gold-hilted
sword that hung at the young man's side. He

drew back the goblet.

"That sword!" he cried; "how came you by it?"

"It was my father's sword," replied Theseus, with a tremulous voice. "These were his sandals. My dear mother (her name is Æthra) told me his story while I was yet a little child. But it is only a month since I grew strong enough to lift the heavy stone and take the sword and sandals from beneath it, and come to Athens to seek my father."

"My son! my son!" cried King Ægeus, flinging away the fatal goblet and tottering down from the throne to fall into the arms of Theseus. "Yes, these are Æthra's eyes. It is my son."

I have quite forgotten what became of the king's nephews. But when the wicked Medea saw this new turn of affairs, she hurried out of the room, and going to her private chambers, lost no time in setting her enchantments at work. In a few moments, she heard a great noise of hissing snakes outside of the chamber window; and, behold! there was her fiery chariot and four huge winged serpents, wriggling and twisting in the air, flourishing their tails higher than the top of the palace, and all ready to set off on an aerial journey. Medea stayed only long enough to take her son with her, and to steal the crown jewels, together with the king's best robes, and whatever other valuable things she could lay hands on; and getting into the chariot, she whipped up the snakes and ascended high over the city.

The king, hearing the hiss of the serpents, scrambled as fast as he could to the window, and cried out to the abominable enchantress never to come back. The whole people of Athens, too, who had run out of doors to see this wonderful spectacle, set up a shout of joy at the prospect of getting rid of her. Medea, almost bursting with rage, uttered precisely such a hiss as one of her own snakes, only ten times more venemous and spiteful; and glaring fiercely out of the blaze of the chariot, she shook her hands over the multitude below, as if she were scattering a million curses among them. In so doing, however, she unintentionally let fall about five hundred diamonds of the first water, together with a thousand great pearls, and two thousand emeralds, rubies, sapphires, opals, and topazes, to which she had helped herself out of the king's strong box. All these came pelting down, like a shower of many-colored hailstones, upon the heads of grown people and children, who forthwith gathered them up, and carried them back to the palace. But King Ægeus told them that they were welcome to the whole, and to twice as many more, if he had them, for the sake of his delight at finding his son, and losing the wicked Medea. And, indeed, if you had seen how hateful was her last look, as the flaming chariot flew upward, you would not have wondered that both king and people should think her departure a good riddance.

And now Prince Theseus was taken into great favor by his royal father. The old king was never weary of having him sit beside him on his throne (which was quite wide enough for two), and of hearing him tell about his deaf mother, and his childhood, and his many boyish efforts to lift the ponderous stone. Theseus, however, was much too brave and active a young man to be willing to spend all his time in relating things which had already happened. His ambition was to perform other and more heroic deeds, which should be better worth telling in prose and verse. Nor had he been long in Athens before he caught and chained a terrible bull, and made a public show of him, greatly to the wonder and admiration of good King AEgeus and his subjects. But pretty soon, he undertook an affair that made all his foregone adventures seem like mere boy's play. The occasion of it was as follows:

One morning, when Prince Theseus awoke, he fancied that he must have had a very sorrowful dream, and that it was still running in his mind, even now that his eyes were open. For it appeared as if the air was full of a melancholy wail; and when he listened more attentively, he could hear sobs and groans and screams of woe, mingled with deep, quiet sighs, which came from the king's palace and from the streets and from the temples and from every habitation in the city. And all these mournful noises, issuing out of thousands of separate hearts, united themselves into the one great sound of affliction which had startled Theseus from slumber. He put on his clothes as quickly as he could (not forgetting his sandals and gold-hilted sword), and hastening to the king, inquired what it all meant.

"Alas! my son," quoth King AEgeus, heaving a long sigh, "here is a very lamentable matter in hand! This is the woefullest anniversary in the whole year. It is the day when we annually draw lots to see which of the youths and maidens of Athens shall go to be devoured by the horrible Minotaur!"

"The Minotaur!" exclaimed Prince Theseus; and like a brave young prince as he was, he put his hand to the hilt of his sword. "What kind of monster may that be? Is it not possible, at the risk of one's life, to slay him?"

But King AEgeus shook his venerable head, and to convince Theseus that it was quite a hopeless case, he gave him an explanation of the whole affair. It seems that in the island of Crete there lived a certain dreadful monster, called a Minotaur, which was shaped partly like a man and partly like a bull, and was altogether such a hideous sort of creature that it is really disagreeable to think of him. If he were suffered to exist at all, it should have been on some desert island, or in the duskiness of some deep cavern where nobody would ever be tormented by his abominable aspect. But King Minos, who reigned over Crete, laid out a vast deal of money in building a habitation for the Minotaur, and took great care of his health and comfort, merely for mischief's sake. A few years before this time, there had been a war between the city of Athens and the island of Crete, in which the Athenians were beaten, and compelled to beg for peace. No peace could they obtain, however, except on condition that they should send seven young men and seven maidens, every year, to be devoured by the pet monster of the cruel King Minos. For three years past, this previous calamity had been borne. And the sobs and groans and shrieks with which the city was now filled, were caused by the people's woe, because the fatal day had come again, when the fourteen victims were to be chosen by lot; and the old people feared lest their sons or daughters might be taken and the youths and damsels dreaded lest they themselves might be destined to glut the ravenous maw of that detestable man-brute.

But when Theseus heard the story, he straightened himself up, so that he seemed taller than ever before; and as for his face, it was indignant, despiteful, bold, tender, and compassionate, all in one look.

"Let the people of Athens, this year, draw lots for only six young men, instead of seven," said he. "I will myself be the seventh; and let the Minotaur devour me, if he can!"

"O my dear son," cried King Ægeus, "why should you expose yourself to this horrible fate? You are a royal prince, and have a right to hold yourself above the destinies of common men."

"It is because I am a prince, your son, and the rightful heir of your kingdom, that I freely take upon me the calamity of your subjects," answered Theseus. "And you, my father, being king over this people, and answerable to Heaven for their welfare, are bound to sacrifice what is dearest to you, rather than that the son or daughter of the poorest citizen should come to any harm."

The old king shed tears and besought Theseus not to leave him desolate in his old age, more especially as he had but just begun to know the happiness of possessing a good and valiant son. Theseus, however, felt that he was in the right, and therefore would not give up his resolution. But he assured his father that he did not intend to be eaten up, unresistingly, like a sheep, and that, if the Minotaur devoured him, it should not be without a battle for his dinner. And finally, since he could not help it, King Ægeus consented to let him go. So a vessel was got ready and rigged with black sails; and Theseus, with six other young men and seven tender and beautiful damsels, came down to the harbor to embark. A sorrowful multitude accompanied them to the shore. There was the poor old king, too, leaning on his son's arm, and looking as if his single heart held all the grief of Athens.

Just as Prince Theseus was going on board, his father bethought himself of one last word to say.

"My beloved son," said he, grasping the prince's hand, "you observe that the sails of this vessel are black· as indeed they ought to be, since it goes upon ᴜ voyage of sorrow and despair. Now, being weighed down with infirmities, I know not whether I can survive till the vessel shall return. But, as long as I do live, I shall creep daily to the top of yonder cliff, to watch if there be a sail upon the sea. And, dearest Theseus, if by some happy chance you should escape the jaws of the Minotaur, then tear down those dismal sails and hoist others that shall be bright as the sunshine. Beholding them on the horizon, myself and all the people will know that you are coming back victorious, and will welcome you with such a festal uproar as Athens never heard before."

Theseus promised that he would do so. Then, going on board, the mariners trimmed the vessel's black sails to the wind, which blew faintly off the shore, being pretty much made up of the sighs that everybody kept pouring forth on this melancholy occasion. But by and by, when they had got fairly out to sea, there came a stiff breeze from the northwest, and drove them along as merrily over the white-capped waves as if they had been going on the most delightful errand imaginable. And though it was a sad business enough, I rather question whether fourteen young people, without any old persons to keep them in order, could continue to spend the whole time of the voyage in being miserable. There had been some few dances upon the undulating deck, I suspect, and some hearty bursts of laughter and other such unseasonable merriment among the victims before the high, blue mountains of Crete began to show themselves among the far-off clouds. That sight, to be sure, made them all very grave again.

Theseus stood among the sailors gazing eagerly toward the land; although, as yet, it seemed hardly more substantial than the clouds, amidst which the mountains were looming up. Once or twice he fancied that he saw a glare of some bright object, a long way off, flinging a gleam across the waves.

"Did you see that flash of light?" he inquired of the master of the vessel.

"No, prince; but I have seen it before," answered the master. "It came from Talus, I suppose."

As the breeze came fresher just then, the master was busy with trimming his sails, and had no more time to answer questions. But, while the vessel flew faster and faster toward Crete, Theseus was astonished to behold a human figure, gigantic in size, which appeared to be striding with a measured movement along the margin of the island. It stepped from cliff to cliff, and sometimes from one headland to another, while the sea foamed and thundered on the shore beneath, and dashed its jets of spray over the giant's feet. What was still more remarkable, whenever the sun shone on this huge figure, it flickered and glimmered; its vast countenance, too, had a metallic luster and threw great flashes of splendor through the air. The folds of its garments, morever, instead of waving in the wind, fell heavily over its limbs, as if woven of some kind of metal.

The nigher the vessel came, the more Theseus wondered what this immense giant could be, and whether it actually had life or no. Though it walked, and made other life-like motions, there yet was a kind of jerk in its gait, which, together with its brazen aspect, caused the young prince to suspect that it was no true giant, but only a wonderful piece of machinery. The figure looked all the more terrible because it carried an enormous brass club on its shoulder.

"What is this wonder?" Theseus asked the master of the vessel, who was now at leisure to answer him.

"It is Talus, the Man of Brass," said the master.

"And is he a live giant, or a brazen image?" asked Theseus.

"That, truly," replied the master, "is the point which has always perplexed me. Some say, indeed, that this Talus was hammered out for King Minos by Vulcan himself, the skilfulest of all workers in metal. But who ever saw a brazen image that had sense enough to walk round an island three times a day, as this giant walks round the island of Crete, challenging every vessel that comes nigh the shore? And, on the other hand, what living thing, unless his sinews were made of brass, would not be weary of marching eighteen hundred miles in the twenty-four hours, as Talus does, without ever sitting down to rest? He is a puzzler, take him how you will."

Still the vessel went bounding onward; and now Theseus could hear the brazen clangor of the giant's footsteps, as he trod heavily upon the sea-beaten rocks, some of which were seen to crack and crumble into the foamy waves beneath his weight. As they approached the entrance of the port, the giant straddled clear across it, with a foot firmly planted on each headland, and uplifting his club to such a height that its butt end was hidden in a cloud, he stood in that formidable posture, with the sun gleaming all over his metallic surface. There seemed nothing else to be expected but that, the next moment, he would fetch his great club down, slam bang, and smash the vessel into a thousand pieces, without heeding how many innocent people he might destroy; for there is seldom any mercy in a giant, you know, and quite as little in a piece of brass clockwork. But just when Theseus and his companions thought the blow was coming, the brazen lips unclosed themselves, and the figure spoke.

"Whence come you, strangers?"

And when the ringing voice ceased, there was just such a reverberation as you may have heard within a great church bell, for a moment or two after the stroke of the hammer.

"From Athens!" shouted the master in reply.

"On what errand?" thundered the Man of Brass.

And he whirled his club aloft more threateningly than ever, as if he were about to smite them with a thunder-stroke right amidships, because Athens, so little while ago, had been at war with Crete.

"We bring the seven youths and the seven maidens," answered the master, "to be devoured by the Minotaur!"

"Pass!" cried the brazen giant.

That one loud word rolled all about the sky, while again there was a booming reverberation within the figure's breast. The vessel glided between the headlands of the port, and the giant resumed his march. In a few moments, this wondrous sentinel was far away, flashing in the distant sunshine and revolving with immense strides around the island of Crete, as it was his never-ceasing task to do.

No sooner had they entered the harbor than a party of the guards of King Minos came down to the waterside, and took charge of the fourteen young men and damsels. Surrounded by these armed warriors, Prince Theseus and his companions were led to the king's palace, and ushered into his presence. Now, Minos was a stern and pitiless king. If the figure that guarded Crete was made of brass, then the monarch, who ruled over it, might be thought to have a still harder metal in his breast, and might have been called a man of iron. He bent his shaggy brows upon the poor Athenian victims. Any other mortal, beholding their fresh and tender beauty and their innocent looks, would have felt himself sitting on thorns until he had made every soul of them happy, by bidding them go free as the summer wind. But this immitigable Minos cared only to examine whether they were plump enough to satisfy the Minotaur's appetite. For my part, I wish he himself had been the only victim; and the monster would have found him a pretty tough one.

One after another, King Minos called these pale, frightened youths and sobbing maidens to his footstool, gave them each a poke in the ribs with his scepter (to try whether they were in good flesh or no), and dismissed them with a nod to his guards. But when his eyes rested on Theseus, the king looked at him more attentively, because his face was calm and brave.

"Young man," asked he, with his stern voice, "are you not appalled at the certainty of being devoured by this terrible Minotaur?"

"I have offered my life in a good cause," answered Theseus, "and therefore I give it freely and gladly. But thou, King Minos, art thou not thyself appalled, who, year after year, hast perpetrated this dreadful wrong, by giving seven innocent youths and as many maidens to be devoured by a monster? Dost thou not tremble, wicked king, to turn thine eyes inward on thine own heart? Sitting there on thy golden throne, and in thy robes of majesty, I tell thee to thy face, King Minos, thou art a more hideous monster than the Minotaur himself!"

"Aha! do you think me so?" cried the king, laughing in his cruel way. "Tomorrow, at breakfast time, you shall have an opportunity of judging which is the greater monster, the Minotaur or the king! Take them away, guards; and let this free-spoken youth be the Minotaur's first morsel!"

Near the king's throne (though I had no time to tell you so before) stood his daughter Ariadne. She was a beautiful and tender-hearted maiden, and looked at these poor doomed captives with very different feelings from those of the iron-breasted King Minos. She really wept, indeed, at the idea of how much human happiness would be needlessly thrown away, by giving so many young people, in the first bloom and rose blossom of their lives, to be eaten up by a creature who, no doubt, would have preferred a fat ox, or even a large pig, to the plumpest of them. And when she beheld the brave spirited figure of Prince Theseus bearing himself so calmly in his terrible peril, she grew a hundred times more pitiful than before. As the guards were taking him away, she flung herself at the king's feet, and besought him to set all the captives free, and especially this one young man.

"Peace, foolish girl!" answered King Minos. "What hast thou to do with an affair like this? It is a matter of state policy, and therefore quite beyond thy weak comprehension. Go water thy flowers, and think no more of these Athenian caitiffs, whom the Minotaur shall as certainly eat up for breakfast as I will eat a partridge for my supper."

So saying, the king looked cruel enough to devour Theseus and all the rest of the captives, himself, had there been no Minotaur to save him the trouble. As he would hear not another word in their favor, the prisoners were now led away, and clapped into a dungeon, where the jailer advised them to go to sleep as soon as possible, because the Minotaur was in the habit of calling for breakfast early. The seven maidens and six of the young men soon sobbed themselves to slumber. But Theseus was not like them. He felt conscious that he was wiser and braver and stronger than his companions, and that therefore he had the responsibility of all their lives upon him, and must consider whether there was no way to save them, even in this last extremity. So he kept himself awake, and paced to and fro across the gloomy dungeon in which they were shut up.

Just before midnight, the door was softly unbarred, and the gentle Ariadne showed herself, with a torch in her hand.

"Are you awake, Prince Theseus?" she whispered.

"Yes," answered Theseus. "With so little time to live, I do not choose to waste any of it in sleep."

"Then follow me," said Ariadne, "and tread softly."

What had become of the jailer and the guards, Theseus never knew. But, however that might be, Ariadne opened all the doors, and led him forth from the darksome prison into the pleasant moonlight.

"Theseus," said the maiden, "you can now get on board your vessel and sail away for Athens."

"No," answered the young man; "I will never leave Crete unless I can first slay the Minotaur, and save my poor companions, and deliver Athens from this cruel tribute."

"I knew that this would be your resolution," said Ariadne.

"Come, then, with me, brave Theseus. Here is your own sword, which the guards deprived you of. You will need it; and pray Heaven you may use it well."

Then she led Theseus along by the hand until they came to a dark, shadowy grove, where the moonlight wasted itself on the tops of the trees, without shedding hardly so much as a glimmering beam upon their pathway. After going a good way through this obscurity, they reached a high marble wall, which was overgrown with creeping plants, that made it shaggy with their verdure. The wall seemed to have no door nor any windows, but rose up, lofty and massive and mysterious, and was neither to be clambered over, nor, so far as Theseus could perceive, to be passed through. Nevertheless, Ariadne did but press one of her soft little fingers against a particular block of marble, and, though it looked as solid as any other part of the wall, it yielded to her touch, disclosing an entrance just wide enough to admit them. They crept through, and the marble stone swung back into its place.

"We are now," said Ariadne, "in the famous labyrinth which Dædalus built before he made himself a pair of wings and flew away from our island like a bird. That Dædalus was a very cunning workman; but of all his artful contrivances, this labyrinth is the most wondrous. Were we to take but a few steps from the doorway, we might wander about all our lifetime and never find it again. Yet in the very center of this labyrinth is the Minotaur; and, Theseus, you must go thither and seek him."

"But how shall I ever find him," asked Theseus, "if the labyrinth so bewilders me as you say it will?"

Just as he spoke, they heard a rough and very disagreeable roar, which greatly resembled the lowing of a fierce bull, but yet had some sort of sound like the human voice. Theseus even fancied a rude articulation in it, as if the creature that uttered it were trying to shape his hoarse breath into words. It was at some distance, however, and he really could not tell whether it sounded most like a bull's roar or a man's harsh voice.

"That is the Minotaur's noise," whispered Ariadne, closely grasping the hand of Theseus, and pressing one of her own hands to her heart, which was all in a tremble. "You must follow that sound through the windings of the labyrinth, and, by and by, you will find him. Stay! Take the end of this silken string; I will hold the other end; and then, if you win the victory, it will lead you again to this spot. Farewell, brave Theseus."

The young man took the end of the silken string in his left hand, and his gold-hilted sword, ready drawn from its scabbard, in the other, and trod boldly into the inscrutable labyrinth. How this labyrinth was built is more than I can tell you, but so cunningly contrived a mizmaze was never seen in the world, before nor since. There can be nothing else so intricate, unless it were the brain of a man like Dædalus, who planned it, or the heart of any ordinary man; which last, to be sure, is ten times as great a mystery as the labyrinth of Crete. Theseus had not taken five steps before he lost sight of Ariadne; and in five more his head was growing dizzy. But still he went on, now creeping through a low arch, now ascending a flight of steps, now in one crooked passage and now in another, with here a door opening before him and there one banging behind, until it really seemed as if the walls spun round, and whirled him round along with them. And all the while, through these hollow avenues, now nearer, now farther off again, resounded the cry of the Minotaur; and the sound was so fierce, so cruel, so ugly, so like a bull's roar, and withal so like a human voice that the brave heart of Theseus grew angrier at every step; for he felt it an insult to the moon and sky and to our affectionate and simple Mother Earth, that such a monster should have the audacity to exist.

As he passed onward, the clouds gathered over the moon and the labyrinth grew so dusky that Theseus could no longer discern the bewilderment through which he was passing. He would have felt quite lost and utterly hopeless of ever walking again in a straight path, if, every little while, he had not been conscious of a gentle twitch at the silken cord. Then he knew that the tender-hearted Ariadne was still holding the other end, and that she was fearing for him and hoping for him and giving him just as much of her sympathy as if she were close by his side. Oh, indeed, I can assure you, there was a vast deal of human sympathy running along that slender thread of silk. But still he followed the dreadful roar of the Minotaur, which now grew louder and louder and finally so very loud that Theseus fully expected to come close upon him, at every new zigzag and wriggle of the path. And at last, in an open space, at the very center of the labyrinth, he did discern the hideous creature.

Sure enough, what an ugly monster it was! Only his horned head belonged to a bull; and yet, somehow or other, he looked like a bull all over, preposterously waddling on his hind legs; or, if you happened to view him in another way, he seemed wholly a man, and all the more monstrous for being so. And there he was, the wretched thing, with no society, no companion, no kind of mate, living only to do mischief, and incapable of knowing what affection means. Theseus hated him and shuddered at him, and yet could not but be sensible of some sort of pity; and all the more, the uglier and more detestable the creature was. He kept striding to and fro in a solitary frenzy of rage continually emitting a hoarse roar, which was oddly mixed with half-shaped words; and, after listening a while, Theseus understood that the Minotaur was saying to himself how miserable he was and how hungry and how he hated everybody and how he longed to eat up the human race alive.

Ah, the bullheaded villain! And, oh, my good little people, you will perhaps see, one of these days, as I do now, that every human being who suffers anything evil to get into his nature, or to remain there, is a kind of Minotaur, an enemy of his fellow creatures, and separated from all good companionship, as this poor monster was.

Was Theseus afraid? By no means, my dear auditors. What? A hero like Theseus afraid! Not had the Minotaur had twenty bull's heads instead of one. Bold as he was, however, I rather fancy that it strengthened his valiant heart, just at this crisis, to feel a tremulous twitch at the silken cord, which he was still holding in his left hand. It was as if Ariadne were giving him all her might and courage; and, much as he already had, and little as she had to give, it made his own seem twice as much. And to confess the honest truth, he needed the whole; for now the Minotaur turning suddenly about, caught sight of Theseus, and instantly lowered his horribly sharp horns, exactly as a mad bull does when he means to rush against an enemy. At the same time, he belched forth a tremendous roar, in which there was something like the words of human language, but all disjointed and shaken to pieces by passing through the gullet of a miserably enraged brute.

Theseus could only guess what the creature

intended to say, and that rather by his gestures than his words; for the Minotaur's horns were sharper than his wits, and of a great deal more service to him than his tongue. But probably this was the sense of what he uttered:

"Ah, wretch of a human being! I'll stick my horns through you, and toss you fifty feet high, and eat you up the moment you come down."

"Come on then, and try it!" was all that Theseus deigned to reply; for he was far too magnanimous to assault his enemy with insolent language.

Without more words on either side, there ensued the most awful fight between Theseus and the Minotaur that ever happened beneath the sun or moon. I really know not how it might have turned out, if the monster, in his first headlong rush against Theseus, had not missed him by a hair's-breadth, and broken one of his horns short off against the stone wall. On this mishap, he bellowed so all the inhabitants of Crete mistook the noise for an uncommonly heavy thunder-storm. Smarting with the pain, he galloped around the open space in so ridiculous a way that Theseus laughed at it long afterwards, though not precisely at the moment. After this, the two antagonists stood valiantly up to each other, and fought sword to horn, for a long while. At last, the Minotaur made a run at Theseus, grazed his left side with his horn, and flung him down; and thinking that he had stabbed him to the heart, he cut a great caper in the air, opened his bull mouth from ear to ear, and prepared to snap Theseus' head off. But Theseus by this time had leaped up and caught the monster off his guard. Fetching a sword stoke at him with all his force,

"The giant straddled clear across the port."

"There ensued the most awful fight between Theseus and the Minotaur that ever happened beneath the sun and the moon."

he hit him fair upon the neck, and made his bull head skip six yards from his human body, which fell down flat upon the ground.

The battle was now ended. Immediately the moon shone out as brightly as if all the troubles of the world and all the wickedness and the ugliness that infest human life, were past and gone forever. And Theseus, as he leaned on his sword, taking breath, felt another twitch of the silken cord; for all through the terrible encounter he had held it fast in his left hand. Eager to let Ariadne know of his success, he followed the guidance of the thread, and soon found himself at the entrance of the labyrinth.

"Thou hast slain the monster," cried Ariadne, clasping her hands.

"Thanks to thee, dear Ariadne," answered Theseus, "I return victorious."

"Then," said Ariadne, "we must quickly summon thy friends, and get them and thyself on board the vessel before dawn. If morning finds thee here, my father will avenge the Minotaur."

To make my story short, the poor captives were awakened, and, hardly knowing whether it was not a joyful dream, were told what Theseus had done, and that they must set sail for Athens before daybreak. Hastening down to the vessel, they all clambered on board, except Prince Theseus, who lingered behind them, on the strand, holding Ariadne's hand clasped in his own.

"Dear maiden," said he, "thou wilt surely go with us. Thou art too gentle and sweet a child for such an iron-hearted father as King Minos. He cares no more for thee than a granite rock cares for the little flower that grows in one of its crevices. But my father, King Ægeus, and my dear mother, AEthra, and all the fathers and mothers in Athens and all the sons and daughters too, will love and honor thee as their benefactress. Come with us, then; for King Minos will be very angry when he knows what thou hast done."

Now, some low-minded people, who pretend to tell the story of Theseus and Ariadne, have the face to say that this royal and honorable maiden did really flee away, under cover of the night, with the young stranger whose life she had preserved. They say, too, that Prince Theseus (who would have died sooner than wrong the meanest creature in the world) ungratefully deserted Ariadne, on a solitary island, where the vessel touched on its voyage to Athens. But, had the noble Theseus heard these falsehoods, he would have served their slanderous authors as he served the Minotaur! Here is what Ariadne answered, when the brave Prince of Athens besought her to accompany him:

"No, Theseus," the maiden said, pressing his hand, and then drawing back a step or two, "I cannot go with you. My father is old and has nobody but myself to love him. Hard as you think his heart is, it would break to lose me. At first King Minos will be angry; but he will soon forgive his only child; and, by and by, he will rejoice, I know, that no more youths and maidens must come from Athens to be devoured by the Minotaur. I have saved you, Theseus, as much for my father's sake as for your own. Farewell! Heaven bless you!"

All this was so true and so maiden-like and was spoken with so sweet a dignity, that Theseus would have blushed to urge her any longer.

Nothing remained for him, therefore, but to bid Ariadne an affectionate farewell, and go on board the vessel and set sail.

In a few moments the white foam was boiling up before their prow, as Prince Theseus and his companions sailed out of the harbor, with a whistling breeze behind them. Talus, the brazen giant, on his never-ceasing sentinel's march, happened to be approaching that part of the coast; and they saw him, by the glimmering of the moonbeams on his polished surface, while he was yet a great way off. As the figure moved like clockwork, however, and could neither hasten his enormous strides nor retard them, he arrived at the port when they were just beyond the reach of his club. Nevertheless, straddling from headland to headland, as his custom was, Talus attempted to strike a blow at the vessel, and, overreaching himself, tumbled at full length into the sea, which splashed high over his gigantic shape, as when an iceberg turns a somerset. There he lies yet; and whoever desires to enrich himself by means of brass had better go thither with a diving bell and fish up Talus.

On the homeward voyage the fourteen youths and damsels were in excellent spirits, as you will easily suppose. They spent most of their time in dancing, except when the sidelong breeze made the deck slope too much. In due season they came within sight of the coast of Attica, which was their native country. But here, I am grieved to tell you, happened a sad misfortune.

You will remember (what Theseus unfortunately forgot) that his father, King Ægeus, had enjoined it upon him to hoist sunshiny sails, instead of black ones, in case he should overcome

the Minotaur, and return victorious. In the joy of
their success, however, and amidst the sports,
dancing, and other merriment, with which these
young folks wore away the time, they never once
thought whether their sails were black, white, or
rainbow colored, and, indeed, left it entirely to
the mariners whether they had any sails at all.
Thus the vessel returned, like a raven, with the
same sable wings that had wafted her away. But
poor King AEgeus, day after day, infirm as he
was, had clambered to the summit of a cliff that
overhung the sea, and there sat watching for
Prince Theseus, homeward bound; and no sooner
did he behold the fatal blackness of the sails,
then he concluded that his dear son, whom he
loved so much, and felt so proud of, had been
eaten by the Minotaur. He could not bear the
thought of living any longer; so, first flinging his
crown and scepter into the sea (useless baubles
that they were to him now!) King AEgeus merely
stooped forward, and fell headlong over the cliff,
and was drowned, poor soul, in the waves that
foamed at its base!

This was melancholy news for Prince Theseus,
who, when he stepped ashore, found himself king
of all the country, whether he would or no; and
such a turn of fortune was enough to make any
young man feel very much out of spirits. However, he sent for his dear mother to Athens, and,
by taking her advice in matters of state, became
a very excellent monarch and was greatly
beloved by his people.

The Pygmies

A GREAT while ago, when the world was full of wonders, there lived an earth-born Giant named Antæus, and a million or more of curious little earth-born people, who were called Pygmies. This Giant and these Pygmies being children of the same mother (that is to say, our good old Grandmother Earth), were all brethren, and dwelt together in a very friendly and affectionate manner, far, far off, in the middle of hot Africa. The pygmies were so small, and there were so many sandy deserts and such high mountains between them and the rest of mankind, that nobody could get a peep at them oftener than once in a hundred years. As for the Giant, being of a very lofty stature, it was easy enough to see him, but safest to keep out of his sight.

Among the Pygmies, I suppose, if one of them grew to the height of six or eight inches, he was reckoned a prodigiously tall man. It must have been very pretty to behold their little cities, with streets two or three feet wide, paved with the smallest pebbles and bordered by habitations about as big as a squirrel's cage. The king's palace attained to the stupendous magnitude of Periwinkle's baby house, and stood in the center of a spacious square, which could hardly have been covered by our hearthrug. Their principal temple, or cathedral, was as lofty as yonder bureau, and was looked upon as a wonderfully sublime and magnificent edifice. All these structures were built neither of stone nor wood. They were neatly plastered together by the Pygmy workmen, pretty much like bird's nests, out of straw, feathers, eggshells, and other small bits of stuff, with stiff clay instead of mortar; and when the hot sun had dried them, they were just as snug and comfortable as a Pygmy could desire.

The country round about was conveniently laid out in fields, the largest of which was nearly of the same extent as one of Sweet Fern's flower beds. Here the Pygmies used to plant wheat and other kinds of grain, which, when it grew up and ripened, overshadowed these tiny people as the pines and the oaks and the walnut and chestnut tress overshadow you and me, when we walk in our own tracts of woodland. At harvest time they were forced to go with their little axes and cut down the grain, exactly as a woodcutter makes a clearing in the forest; and when a stalk of wheat, with its overburdened top, chanced to come crashing down upon an unfortunate Pygmy, it was apt to be a very sad affair. If it did not smash him all to pieces, at least, I am sure, it must have made the poor little fellow's head ache. And oh, my stars! if the fathers and mothers were so small, what must the children and babies have been? A whole family of them might have been put to bed in a shoe, or have crept into an old glove, and played at hide and seek in its thumb and fingers. You might have hidden a year-old baby under a thimble.

Now these funny Pygmies, as I told you before, had a Giant for their neighbor and brother, who was bigger, if possible, than they were little. He was so very tall that he carried a pine tree, which was eight feet through the butt, for a walking stick. It took a far-sighted Pygmy, I can assure you, to discern his summit without the help of a telescope; and sometimes, in misty weather, they could not see his upper half, but only his long legs, which seemed to be striding about by themselves. But at noonday, in a clear atmosphere, when the sun shone brightly over him, the Giant Antæus presented a very grand spectacle. There he used to stand, a perfect mountain of a man, with his great countenance smiling down upon his little brothers, and his one vast eye (which was as big as a cart wheel, and placed right in the center of his forehead) giving a friendly wink to the whole nation at once.

The Pygmies loved to talk with Antæus; and fifty times a day, one or another of them would turn up his head and shout through the hollow of his fists: "Halloo, brother Antæus! How are you, my good fellow?" and when the small, distant squeak of their voices reached his ear, the Giant would make answer, "Pretty well, brother Pygmy, I thank you," in a thunderous roar that would have shaken down the walls of their strongest temple, only that it came from so far aloft.

It was a happy circumstance that Antæus was the Pygmy people's friend; for there was more

strength in his little finger than in ten million of
such bodies as theirs. If he had been as ill-
natured to them as he was to everybody else, he
might have beaten down their biggest city at one
kick and hardly have known that he did it. With
the tornado of his breath, he could have stripped
the roofs from a hundred dwellings and sent
thousands of the inhabitants whirling through the
air. He might have set his immense foot upon a
multitude; and when he took it up again, there
would have been a pitiful sight, to be sure. But
being the son of Mother Earth, as they likewise
were, the Giant gave them his brotherly
kindness, and loved them with as big a love as it
was possible to feel for creatures so very small.
And, on their parts, the Pygmies loved Antæus
with as much affection as their tiny hearts could
hold. He was always ready to do them any good
offices that lay in his power; as, for example,
when they wanted a breeze to turn their wind-
mills, the Giant would set all the sails a-going
with the mere natural respiration of his lungs.
When the sun was too hot, he often sat himself
down and let his shadow fall over the kingdom,
from one frontier to the other; and as for
matters in general, he was wise enough to let the
Pygmies manage their own affairs — which,
after all, is about the best thing that great
people can do for little ones.

In short, as I said before, Antæus loved the
Pygmies and the Pygmies loved Antæus. The
Giant's life being as long as his body was large,
while the lifetime of a Pygmy was but a span,
this friendly intercourse had been going on for
innumerable generations and ages. It was written about in the Pygmy histories, and talked

about in their ancient traditions. The most venerable and white-bearded Pygmy had never heard of a time, even in his greatest of grandfather's days, when the Giant was not their enormous friend. Once, to be sure (as was recorded on an obelisk), Antæus sat down upon about five thousand Pygmies, who were assembled at a military review. But this was one of those unlucky accidents for which nobody is to blame; so that the small folks never took it to heart, and only requested the Giant to be careful forever afterwards to examine the acre of ground where he intended to squat himself.

It is a very pleasant picture to imagine Antæus standing among the Pygmies, like the spire of the tallest cathedral that ever was built, while they ran about like pismires at his feet; and to think that, in spite of their difference in size, there were affection and sympathy between them and him! Indeed, it has always seemed to me that the Giant needed the little people more than the Pygmies needed the Giant. For, unless they had been his neighbors and well-wishers, and, as we may say, his playfellows, Antæus would not have had a single friend in the world. No other being like himself had ever been created. No creature of his own size had ever talked with him, in thunder-like accents face to face. When he stood with his head among the clouds, he was quite alone, and had been so for hundreds of years, and would be so forever. Even if he had met another Giant, Antæus would have fancied the world not big enough for two such vast personages, and, instead of being friends with him, would have fought him till one of the two was killed. But with the Pygmies he was the

most sportive and humorous and merry-hearted
and sweet-tempered old Giant that ever washed
his face in a wet cloud.

His little friends, like all other small people,
had a great opinion of their own importance, and
used to assume quite a patronizing air toward the
Giant.

"Poor creature!" they said one to another. "He
has a very dull time of it, all by himself; and we
ought not to grudge wasting a little of our
precious time to amuse him. He is not half so
bright as we are, to be sure; and, for that reason,
he needs us to look after his comfort and
happiness. Let us be kind to the old fellow.
Why, if Mother Earth had not been very kind to
ourselves, we might all have been Giants too."

On all their holidays, the Pygmies had
excellent sport with Antæus. He often stretched
himself out at full length on the ground, where
he looked like the long ridge of a hill; and it was
a good hour's walk, no doubt, for a short-legged
Pygmy to journey from head to foot of the Giant.
He would lay down his great hand flat on the
grass, and challenge the tallest of them to
clamber upon it and straddle from finger to
finger. So fearless were they that they made
nothing of creeping in among the folds of his
garments. When his head lay sidewise on the
earth, they would march boldly up, and peep into
the great cavern of his mouth, and take it all as
a joke (as indeed it was meant) when Antæus
gave a sudden snap with his jaws, as if he were
going to swallow fifty of them at once. You
would have laughed to see the children dodging in
and out among his hair or swinging from his
beard. It is impossible to tell half of the funny

tricks that they played with their huge comrade; but I do not know that anything was more curious than when a party of boys were seen running races on his forehead, to try which of them could get first round the circle of his one great eye. It was another favorite feat with them to march along the bridge of his nose, and jump down upon his upper lip.

If the truth must be told, they were sometimes as troublesome to the Giant as a swarm of ants or mosquitoes, especially as they had a fondness for mischief, and liked to prick his skin with their little swords and lances, to see how thick and tough it was. But Antæus took it all kindly enough; although, once in a while, when he happened to be sleepy, he would grumble out a peevish word or two, like the muttering of a tempest, and ask them to have done with their nonsense. A great deal oftener, however, he watched their merriment and gambols until his huge, heavy, clumsy wits were completely stirred up by them; and then would he roar out such a tremendous volume of immeasurable laughter, that the whole nation of Pygmies had to put their hands to their ears, else it would certainly have deafened them.

"Ho! ho! ho!" quoth the Giant, shaking his mountainous sides. "What a funny thing it is to be little! If I were not Antæus, I should like to be a Pygmy, just for the joke's sake."

The Pygmies had but one thing to trouble them in the world. They were constantly at war with the cranes, and had always been so, ever since the long-lived Giant could remember. From time to time, very terrible battles had been fought, in which sometimes the little men won the victory and sometimes the cranes. According to some historians, the Pygmies used to go to the battle, mounted on the backs of goats and rams; but such animals as these must have been far too big for Pygmies to ride upon; so that, I rather suppose, they rode on squirrel-back, or rabbit-back, or rat-back, or perhaps got upon hedge-hogs, whose prickly quills would be very terrible to the enemy. However this might be, and whatever creatures the Pygmies rode upon, I do not doubt that they made a formidable appearance, armed with sword and spear and bow and arrow, blowing their tiny trumpet, and shouting their little war cry. They never failed to exhort one another to fight bravely, and recollect that the world had its eyes upon them; although, in simple truth, the only spectator was the Giant Antæus, with his one, great, stupid eye in the middle of his forehead.

When the two armies joined battle, the cranes would rush forward, flapping their wings and stretching out their necks, and would perhaps snatch up some of the Pygmies crosswise in their beaks. Whenever this happened, it was truly an awful spectacle to see those little men of might kicking and sprawling in the air, and at last disappearing down the crane's long crooked throat, swallowed up alive. A hero, you know, must hold himself in readiness for any kind of fate; and doubtless the glory of the thing was a consolation to him, even in the crane's gizzard. If Antæus observed that the battle was going hard against his little allies, he generally stopped laughing, and ran with mile-long strides to their assistance, flourishing his club aloft and shouting at the cranes, who quacked and croaked and retreated as fast as they could. Then the Pygmy army would march homeward in triumph, attributing the victory entirely to their own valor, and to the warlike skill and strategy of whomsoever happened to be captain-general; for a tedious while afterwards, nothing would be heard of but grand processions and public banquets and brilliant illuminations and shows of waxwork, with likenesses of the distinguished officers as small as life.

In the above described warfare, if a Pygmy chanced to pluck out a crane's tail feather, it proved a very great feather in his cap. Once or twice, if you will believe me, a little man was made chief ruler of the nation for no other merit in the world than bringing home such a feather.

But I have now said enough to let you see what a gallant little people these were, and how happily they and their forefathers, for nobody knows how many generations, had lived with the immeasurable Giant Antæus. In the remaining part of the story, I shall tell you of a far more astonishing battle than any that was fought between the Pygmies and the cranes.

One day the mighty Antæus was lolling at full length among his little friends. His pine-tree walking stick lay on the ground, close by his side. His head was in one part of the kingdom, and his feet extended across the boundaries of another part; and he was taking whatever comfort he could get, while the Pygmies scrambled over him, and peeped into his cavernous mouth, and played among his hair. Sometimes, for a minute or two, the Giant dropped asleep, and snored like the rush of a whirlwind. During one of these little bits of slumber a Pygmy chanced to climb upon his shoulder, and took a view around the horizon, as from the summit of a hill; and he beheld something, a long way off, which made him rub the bright specks of his eyes, and look sharper than before. At first he mistook it for a mountain, and wondered how it had grown up so suddenly out of the earth. But soon he saw the mountain move. As it came nearer and nearer, what should it turn out to be but a human shape, not so big as Antæus, it is true, although a very enormous figure, in comparison with Pygmies, and a vast deal bigger than the men whom we see nowadays.

When the Pygmy was quite satisfied that his eyes had not deceived him, he scampered, as fast as his legs would carry him to the Giant's ear, and stooping over its cavity, shoulted lustily into it:

"Halloo, brother Antæus! Get up this minute and take your pine-tree walking stick in your hand. Here comes another Giant to have a tussle with you."

"Poh, poh!" grumbled Antæus, only half awake. "None of your nonsense, my little fellow! Don't you see I'm sleepy? There is not a Giant on earth for whom I would take the trouble to get up."

But the Pygmy looked again, and now perceived that the stranger was coming directly toward the prostrate form of Antæus. With every step he looked less like a blue mountain, and more like an immensely large man. He was soon so nigh that there could be no possible mistake about the matter. There he was, with the sun flaming on his golden helmet and flashing from his polished breastplate; he had a sword by his side and a lion's skin over his back, and on his right shoulder he carried a club, which looked bulkier and heavier than the pine-tree walking stick of Antæus.

By this time, the whole nation of Pygmies had seen the new wonder, and a million of them set up a shout, all together; so that it really made quite an audible squeak.

"Get up, Antæus! Bestir yourself, you lazy old Giant! Here comes another Giant, as strong as you are, to fight with you."

"Nonsense, nonsense!" growled the sleepy Giant. "I'll have my nap out, come who may."

Still the stranger drew nearer; and now the Pygmies could plainly discern that, if his stature were less lofty than the Giant's, yet his shoulders were even broader. And, in truth, what a pair of shoulders they must have been! As I told you, a long while ago, they once upheld the sky. The Pygmies, being ten times as vivacious as their great numskull of a brother, could not abide the Giant's slow movements, and were determined to have him on his feet. So they kept shouting to him, and even went so far as to prick him with their swords.

"Get up, get up, get up!" they cried. "Up with you, lazy bones! The strange Giant's club is bigger than your own, his shoulders are the broadest, and we think him the stronger of the two."

Antæus could not endure to have it said that any mortal was half so mighty as himself. This latter remark of the Pygmies pricked him deeper than their swords; and, sitting up, in rather a sulky humor, he gave a gape of several yards wide, rubbed his eye, and finally turned his stupid head in the direction whither his little friends were eagerly pointing.

No sooner did he set eye on the stranger, than, leaping on his feet, and seizing his walking stick, he strode a mile or two to meet him; all the while brandishing the sturdy pine tree, so that it whistled through the air.

"Who are you?" thundered the Giant. "And what do you want in my dominions?"

There was one strange thing about Antæus, of which I have not yet told you, lest, hearing of so many wonders all in a lump, you might not believe much more than half of them. You are to know, then, that whenever this redoubtable Giant touched the ground, either with his hand, his foot, or any other part of his body, he grew stronger than ever he had been before. The Earth, you remember, was his mother, and was very fond of him, as being almost the biggest of her children; and so she took this method of keeping him always in full vigor. Some persons affirm that he grew ten times stronger at every touch; others say that it was only twice as strong. But only think of it! Whenever Antæus took a walk, supposing it were but ten miles, and that he stepped a hundred yards at a stride, you may try to cipher out how much mightier he was, on sitting down again, than when he first started. And whenever he flung himself on the earth to take a little repose, even if he got up the very next instant, he would be as strong as exactly ten just such Giants as his former self. It was well for the world that Antæus happened to be of a sluggish disposition, and liked ease better than exercise; for, if he had frisked about like the Pygmies and touched the earth as often as they did, he would long ago have been strong enough to pull down the sky about people's ears. But these great lubberly fellows resemble mountains, not only in bulk, but in their disinclination to move.

Any other mortal man, except the very one whom Antæus had now encountered, would have been half frightened to death by the Giant's ferocious aspect and terrible voice. But the stranger did not seem at all disturbed. He carelessly lifted his club and balanced it in his hand, measuring Antæus with his eye, from head to foot, not as if wonder-smitten at his stature, but as if he had seen a great many Giants before, and this was by no means the biggest of them. In fact, if the Giant had been no bigger than the Pygmies (who stood pricking up their ears, and looking and listening to what was going forward), the stranger could not have been less afraid of him.

"Who are you, I say?" roared Antæus again. "What's your name? What do you come hither? Speak, you vagabond, or I'll try the thickness of your skull with my walking stick."

"You are a very discourteous Giant," answered the stranger quietly, "and I shall probably have to teach you a little civility before we part. As for my name, it is Hercules. I have come hither because this is my most convenient road to the garden of the Hesperides, whither I am going to get three of the golden apples for King Eurystheus."

"Caitiff, you shall go no farther!" bellowed Antæus, putting on a grimmer look than before; for he had heard of the mighty Hercules, and hated him because he was said to be so strong. "Neither shall you go back whence you came!"

"How will you prevent me," asked Hercules, "from going whither I please?"

"By hitting you a rap with this pine tree here," shouted Antæus, scowling so that he made himself the ugliest monster in Africa. "I am fifty times stronger than you; and, now that I stamp my foot upon the ground, I am five hundred times stronger! I am ashamed to kill such a puny little dwarf as you seem to be. I will make a slave of you, and you shall likewise be the slave of my brethren here, the Pygmies. Throw down your club and your other weapons; and as for that lion's skin, I intend to have a pair of gloves made of it."

"Come and take it off my shoulders, then," answered Hercules, lifting his club.

Then the Giant, grinning with rage, strode tower-like toward the stranger (ten times strengthened at every step), and fetched a monstrous blow at him with his pine tree, which Hercules caught upon his club; and being more skilful than Antæus, he paid him back such a rap upon the sconce, that down tumbled the great lumbering man-mountain, flat upon the ground. The poor little Pygmies (who really never dreamed that anybody in the world was half so strong as their brother Antæus) were a good deal dismayed at this. But no sooner was the Giant down than up he bounced again, with tenfold might, and such a furious visage as was horrible to behold. He aimed another blow at Hercules, but struck awry, being blinded with wrath, and only hit his poor innocent Mother Earth, who groaned and trembled at the stroke. His pine tree went so deep into the ground and stuck there so fast, that before Antæus could get it out, Hercules brought down his club across his shoulders with a mighty thwack, which made the Giant roar as if all sorts of intolerable noises had come screeching and rumbling out of his immeasurable lungs in that one cry. Away it went, over mountains and valleys, and, for aught I know, was heard on the other side of the African deserts.

As for the Pygmies, their capital city was laid in ruins by the concussion and vibration of the air; and, though there was uproar enough without their help, they all set up a shriek out of three millions of little throats, fancying no doubt, that they swelled the Giant's bellow by at least ten times as much. Meanwhile, Antæus had scrambled upon his feet again, and pulled his pine tree out of the earth; and, all a-flame with fury, and more outrageously strong than ever, he ran at Hercules, and brought down another blow.

"This time, rascal," shouted he, "you shall not escape me."

But once more Hercules warded off the stroke with his club, and the Giant's pine tree was shattered into a thousand splinters, most of which flew among the Pygmies, and did them more mischief than I like to think about. Before Antæus could get out of the way, Hercules let drive again, and gave him another knock-down blow, which sent him heels over head, but served only to increase his already enormous and insufferable strength. As for his rage, there is no telling what a fiery furnace it had now got to be. His one eye was nothing but a circle of red flame. Having now no weapons but his fists, he doubled them up (each bigger than a hogshead), smote one against the other, and danced up and down with absolute frenzy, flourishing his immense arms about, as if he meant not merely to kill Hercules, but to smash the whole world to pieces.

"Come on!" roared this thundering Giant. "Let me hit you but one box on the ear and you'll never have the headache again."

Now Hercules (though strong enough, as you already know, to hold the sky up) began to be sensible that he should never win the victory, if he kept on knocking Antæus down; for, by and by, if he hit him such hard blows, the Giant would inevitably, by the help of his Mother Earth, become stronger than the mighty Hercules himself. So, throwing down his club, with which he had fought so many dreadful battles, the hero stood ready to receive his antagonist with naked arms.

"Step forward," cried he. "Since I've broken your pine tree, we'll try which is the better man at a wrestling match."

"Aha! then I'll soon satisfy you," shouted the Giant; for, if there was one thing on which he prided himself more than another, it was his skill in wrestling. "Villain, I'll fling you where you can never pick yourself up again."

On came Antæus, hopping and capering with the scorching heat of his rage, and getting new vigor wherewith to wreak his passion every time he hopped. But Hercules, you must understand, was wiser than this numskull of a Giant, and had thought of a way to fight him — huge, earth-born monster that he was — and to conquer him too, in spite of all that his Mother Earth could do for him. Watching his opportunity, as the mad Giant made a rush at him, Hercules caught him round the middle with both hands, lifted him high into the air, and held him aloft overhead.

Just imagine it, my dear little friends! What a spectacle it must have been, to see this monstrous fellow sprawling in the air, face downward, kicking out his long legs and wriggling his whole vast body, like a baby when its father holds it at arm's length toward the ceiling.

But the most wonderful thing was, that as soon as Antæus was fairly off the earth he began to lose the vigor which he had gained by touching it. Hercules very soon perceived that his troublesome enemy was growing weaker, both because he struggled and kicked with less violence, and because the thunder of his big voice subsided into a grumble. The truth was, that unless the Giant touched Mother Earth as often as once in five minutes, not only his overgrown strength, but the very breath of his life, would depart from him. Hercules had guessed this secret; and it may be well for us all to remember it, in case we should ever have to fight a battle with a fellow like Antæus. For these earth-born creatures are only difficult to conquer on their own ground, but may easily be managed if we can contrive to lift them into a loftier and purer region. So it proved with the poor Giant, whom I am really a little sorry for, notwithstanding his uncivil way of treating strangers who came to visit him.

When his strength and breath were quite gone, Hercules gave his huge body a toss, and flung it about a mile off, where it fell heavily, and lay with no more motion than a sand hill. It was too late for the Giant's Mother Earth to help him now; and I should not wonder if his ponderous bones were lying on the same spot to this very day, and were mistaken for those of an uncommonly large elephant.

But, alas me! What a wailing did the poor little Pygmies set up when they saw their enormous brother treated in this terrible manner! If Hercules heard their shrieks, however, he took no notice, and perhaps fancied them only the shrill, plaintive twittering of small birds that had been frightened from their nests by the uproar of the battle between himself and Antæus. Indeed, his thoughts has been so much taken up with the Giant that he had never once looked at the Pygmies, nor even knew that there was such a funny little nation in the world. And now, as he had traveled a long distance, and was also rather weary with his exertions in the fight, he spread out his lion's skin on the ground, and reclining himself upon it, fell fast asleep.

As soon as the Pygmies saw Hercules preparing for a nap, they nodded their little heads at one another, and winked with their little eyes. And when his deep, regular breathing gave them notice that he was asleep, they assembled together in an immense crowd, spreading over a space of about twenty-seven feet square. One of their most eloquent orators (and a valiant warrior enough, besides, though hardly so good at any other weapon as he was with his tongue) climbed upon a toadstool, and, from that elevated position, addressed the multitude. His sentiments were pretty much as follows; or, at all events, something like this was probably the upshot of his speech:

"Tall Pygmies and mighty little men! You and all of us have seen what a public calamity has been brought to pass, and what an insult has here been offered to the majesty of our nation. Yonder lies Antæus, our great friend and brother, slain, within our territory, by a miscreant who took him at disadvantage, and fought him (if fighting it can be called) in a way that neither man or Giant nor Pygmy ever dreamed of fighting, until this hour. And, adding a grievous contumely to the wrong already done us, the miscreant has now fallen asleep as quietly as if nothing were to be dreaded from our wrath. It behooves you, fellow countrymen, to consider in what aspect we shall stand before the world, and what will be the verdict of impartial history, should we suffer these accumulated outrages to go unavenged.

"Antæus was our brother, born of that same beloved parent to whom we owe the thews and sinews, as well as the courageous hearts, which made him proud of our relationship. He was our faithful ally, and fell fighting as much for our national rights and immunities as for his own personal ones. We and our forefathers have dwelt in friendship with him and held affectionate intercourse, as man to man, through immemorial generations. You remember how often our entire people have reposed in his great shadow, and how our little ones have played at hide and seek in the tangles of his hair, and how his mighty footsteps have familiarly gone to and fro among us, and never trodden upon any of our toes. And there lies this dear brother, this sweet and amiable friend, this brave and faithful ally, this virtuous Giant, this blameless and excellent Antæus — dead! Dead! Silent! Powerless! A mere mountain of clay! Forgive my tears! Nay, I behold your own! Were we to drown the world with them, could the world blame us?

"But to resume: Shall we, my countrymen, suffer this wicked stranger to depart unharmed, and triumph in his treacherous victory, among distant communities of the earth?   Shall we not rather compel him to leave his bones here on our soil, by the side of our slain brother's bones, so that while one skeleton shall remain as the everlasting monument of our sorrow, the other shall endure as long, exhibiting to the whole human race a terrible example of Pygmy vengeance?   Such is the question. I put it to you in full confidence of a response that shall be worthy of our national character and calculated to increase, rather than diminish, the glory which our ancestors have transmitted to us, and which we ourselves have proudly vindicated in our warfare with the cranes."

The orator was here interrupted by a burst of irrepressible enthusiasm; every individual Pygmy crying out that the national honor must be preserved at all hazards. He bowed, and making a gesture for silence, wound up his harangue in the following admirable manner:

"It only remains for us, then, to decide whether we shall carry on the war in our national capacity — one united people against a common enemy — or whether some champion, famous in former fights, shall be selected to defy the slayer of our brother Antæus to single combat. In the latter case, though not unconscious that there may be taller men among you, I hereby offer myself for that enviable duty. And, believe me, dear countrymen, whether I live or die, the honor of this great country and the fame bequeathed us by our heroic progenitors shall suffer no diminution in my hands. Never, while I can wield this sword, of which I now fling away the scabbard — never, never, never, even if the crimson hand that slew the great Antæus shall lay me prostrate, like him, on the soil which I give my life to defend."

So saying, this valiant Pygmy drew out his weapon, (which was terrible to behold, being as long as the blade of a penknife) and sent the scabbard whirling over the heads of the multitude. His speech was followed by an uproar of applause, as its patriotism and self-devotion unquestionably deserved; and the shouts and clapping of hands would have been greatly prolonged had they not been rendered quite inaudible by a deep respiration, vulgarly called a snore, from the sleeping Hercules.

It was finally decided that the whole nation of Pygmies should set to work to destroy Hercules; not, be it understood, from any doubt that a single champion would be capable of putting him to the sword, but because he was a public enemy, and all were desirous of sharing in the glory of his defeat. There was a debate whether the national honor did not demand that a herald should be sent with a trumpet, to stand over the ear of Hercules, and, after blowing a blast right into it, to defy him to the combat by formal proclamation. But two or three venerable and sagacious Pygmies, well-versed in state affairs, gave it as their opinion that war already existed, and that it was their rightful privilege to take the enemy by surprise. Moreover, if awakened and allowed to get upon his feet, Hercules might happen to do them a mischief before he could be beaten down again. For, as these sage counselors remarked, the stranger's club was really very big, and had rattled like a thunderbolt against the skull of Antæus. So the Pygmies resolved to set aside all foolish punctilios and assail their antagonist at once.

Accordingly, all the fighting men of the nation took their weapons and went boldly up to Hercules, who still lay fast asleep, little dreaming of the harm which the Pygmies meant to do him. A body of twenty thousand archers marched in front, with their little bows all ready, and the arrows on the string. The same number were ordered to clamber upon Hercules, some with spades to dig his eyes out, and other with bundles of hay and all manner of rubbish, with which they intended to plug up his mouth and nostrils, so that he might perish for lack of breath. These last, however, could by no means perform their appointed duty; inasmuch as the enemy's breath rushed out of his nose in an obstreperous hurricane and whirlwind, which blew the Pygmies away as fast as they came nigh. It was found necessary, therefore, to hit upon some other method of carrying on the war.

After holding a council, the captains ordered their troops to collect sticks, straws, dry weeds, and whatever combustible stuff they could find, and make a pile of it, heaping it high around the head of Hercules. As a great many thousand Pygmies were employed in this task, they soon brought together several bushels of inflammatory matter, and raised so tall a heap, that, mounting on its summit, they were quite upon a level with the sleeper's face. The archers, meanwhile, were stationed within bowshot, with orders to let fly at Hercules the instant that he stirred. Everything being in readiness, a torch was applied to the pile, which immediately burst into flames and soon waxed hot enough to roast the enemy, had he but chosen to lie still. A Pygmy, you know, though so very small, might set the world on fire, just as easily as a Giant could; so that this was certainly the very best way of dealing with their foe, provided they could have kept him quiet while the conflagration was going forward.

But no sooner did Hercules begin to be scorched than up he started, with his hair in a red blaze.

"What's all this?" he cried, bewildered with sleep and staring about him as if he expected to see another Giant.

At that moment the twenty thousand archers twanged their bowstrings and the arrows came whizzing, right into the face of Hercules. But I doubt whether more than half a dozen of them punctured the skin, which was remarkably tough, as you know the skin of a hero has good need to be.

"Villain!" shouted all the Pygmies at once. "You have killed the Giant Antæus, our great brother, and the ally of our nation. We declare bloody war against you and will slay you on the spot."

Surprised at the shrill piping of so many little voices, Hercules, after putting out the conflagration of his hair, gazed all round about, but could see nothing. At last, however, looking narrowly on the ground, he espied the innumerable assemblage of Pygmies at his feet. He stooped down, and taking up the nearest one between his thumb and finger, set him on the palm of his left hand, and held him at a proper distance for examination. It chanced to be the very identical Pygmy who had spoken from the top of the toadstool and had offered himself as a champion to meet Hercules in single combat.

"What in the world, my little fellow," ejaculated Hercules, "may you be?"

"I am your enemy," answered the valiant Pygmy, in his mightiest squeak. "You have slain the enormous Antæus, our brother by the mother's side, and for ages the faithful ally of our illustrious nation. We are determined to put you to death. For my own part, I challenge you to instant battle, on equal ground."

Hercules was so tickled with the Pygmy's big words and warlike gestures, that he burst into a great explosion of laughter and almost dropped the poor little mite of a creature off the palm of his hand, through the ecstasy and convulsion of his merriment.

"Upon my word," said he, "I thought I had seen wonders before today — hydras with nine heads, stags with golden horns, six-legged men, three-headed dogs, giants with furnaces in their stomachs, and nobody knows what besides. But here, on the palm of my hand, stands a wonder that outdoes them all! Your body, my little friend, is about the size of an ordinary man's finger. Pray, how big may your soul be?"

"As big as your own!" said the Pygmy.

Hercules was touched with the little man's dauntless courage, and could not help acknowledging such a brotherhood with him as one hero feels for another.

"My good little people," said he, making a low obeisance to the grand nation, "not for all the world would I do an intentional injury to such brave fellows as you! Your hearts seem to me so exceedingly great, that, upon my honor, I marvel how your small bodies can contain them. I sue for peace, and, as a condition of it, will take five strides and be out of your kingdom at the sixth. Good-by. I shall pick my steps carefully, for fear of treading upon some fifty of you, without knowing it. Ha, ha, ha! Ho, ho, ho! For once, Hercules acknowledges himself vanquished."

Some writers say that Hercules gathered up the whole race of Pygmies in his lion's skin, and carried them home to Greece, for the children of King Eurystheus to play with. But this is a mistake. He left them, one and all, within their own territory, where, for aught I can tell, their descendants are alive to the present day, building their little houses, cultivating their little fields, spanking their little children, waging their little warfare with the cranes, doing their little business, whatever it may be, and reading their little histories of ancient times. In those histories, perhaps, it stands recorded that, a great many centuries ago, the valiant Pygmies avenged the death of the Giant Antæus by scaring away the mighty Hercules.

The Dragon's Teeth

CADMUS, Phœnix, and Cilix, the three sons of King Agenor, and their little sister Europa (who was a very beautiful child) were at play together, near the seashore, in their father's kingdom of Phœnicia. They had rambled to some distance from the palace where their parents dwelt, and were now in a verdant meadow, on one side of which lay the sea, all sparkling and dimpling in the sunshine and murmuring gently against the beach. The three boys were very happy, gathering flowers and twining them into garlands, with which they adorned the little Europa. Seated on the grass, the child was almost hidden under an abundance of buds and blossoms, whence her rosy face peeped merrily out, and, as Cadmus said, was the prettiest of all the flowers.

Just then, there came a splendid butterfly, fluttering along the meadow; and Cadmus, Phœnix, and Cilix set off in pursuit of it, crying out that it was a flower with wings. Europa, who was a little wearied with playing all day long, did not chase the butterfly with her brothers, but sat still where they had left her, and closed her eyes.

For a while she listened to the pleasant murmur of the sea, which was like a voice saying "Hush!" and bidding her go to sleep. But the pretty child, if she slept at all, could not have slept more than a moment, when she heard something trample on the grass, not far from her, and peeping out from the heap of flowers, beheld a snow-white bull.

Whence could this bull have come? Europa and her brothers had been a long time playing in the meadow, and had seen no cattle nor other living thing, either there or on the neighboring hills.

"Brother Cadmus!" cried Europa, starting up out of the midst of the roses and lilies. "Phœnix, Cilix! Where are you all? Help! Help! Come and drive away this bull!"

But her brothers were too far off to hear; especially as the fright took away Europa's voice and hindered her from calling very loudly. So there she stood, with her pretty mouth wide open, as pale as the white lilies that were twisted among the other flowers in her garlands.

Nevertheless, it was the suddenness with which she had perceived the bull, rather than anything frightful in his appearance, that caused Europa so much alarm. On looking at him more attentively, she began to see that he was a beautiful animal and even fancied a particularly amiable expression in his face. As for his breath — the breath of cattle, you know, is always sweet — it was as fragrant as if he had been grazing on no other food than rosebuds, or, at least, the most delicate of clover blossoms. Never before did a bull have such bright and tender eyes and such smooth horns of ivory, as this one. The bull ran little races and capered sportively around the child; so that she quite forgot how big and strong he was, and, from the gentleness and playfulness of his actions, soon came to consider him as innocent a creature as a pet lamb.

Thus, frightened as she at first was, you might by and by have seen Europa stroking the bull's forehead with her small white hand, and taking the garlands off her own head to hang them on his neck and ivory horns. Then she pulled up some blades of grass and he ate them out of her hand, not as if he were hungry, but because he wanted to be friends with the child and took pleasure in eating what she had touched. Well, my stars! was there ever such a gentle, sweet, pretty, and amiable creature as this bull, and ever such a nice playmate for a little girl?

When the animal saw (for the bull had so much intelligence that it is really wonderful to think of) that Europa was no longer afraid of him, he grew overjoyed, and could hardly contain himself for delight. He frisked about the meadow, now here, now there, making sprightly leaps, with as little effort as a bird expends in hopping from twig to twig. Indeed, his motion was as light as if he were flying through the air, and his hoofs seemed hardly to leave their print in the grassy soil over which he trod. With his spotless hue, he resembled a snowdrift, wafted along by the wind. Once he galloped so far away that Europa feared lest she might never see him again; so setting up her childish voice, she called him back.

"Come back, pretty creature!" she cried. "Here is a nice clover blossom."

And then it was delightful to witness the gratitude of this amiable bull. He was so full of joy and thankfulness that he capered higher than ever. He came running and bowed his head before Europa, as if he knew her to be a king's daughter, or else recognized the important truth that a little girl is everybody's queen. And not only did the bull bend his neck, but he absolutely knelt down at her feet and made such intelligent nods and other inviting gestures, that Europa understood what he meant just as well as if he had put it in so many words.

"Come, dear child," was what he wanted to say, "let me give you a ride on my back."

At the first thought of such a thing, Europa drew back. But then she considered in her wise little head that there could be no possible harm in taking just one gallop on the back of this docile and friendly animal, who would certainly set her down the very instant she desired it. And how it would surprise her brothers to see her riding across the green meadow! What merry times they might have, either taking turns for a gallop or clambering on the gentle creature, all four children together, and careering round the field with shouts of laughter that would be heard as far off as King Agenor's palace!

"I think I will do it," said the child to herself.

And, indeed, why not? She cast a glance around, and caught a glimpse of Cadmus, Phœnix, and Cilix, who were still in pursuit of the butterfly, almost at the other end of the meadow. It would be the quickest way of rejoining them, to get upon the white bull's back. She came a step nearer to him, therefore; and — sociable creature that he was — he showed so much joy at this mark of her confidence that the child could not find it in her heart to hestitate any longer. Making one bound (for this little

princess was as active as a squirrel), there sat
Europa on the beautiful bull, holding an ivory
horn in each hand, lest she should fall off.

"Softly, pretty bull, softly!" she said, rather
frightened at what she had done. "Do not gallop
too fast."

Having got the child on his back, the animal
gave a leap into the air and came down so like a
feather that Europa did not know when his hoofs
touched the ground. He then began a race to
that part of the flowery plain where her three
brothers were, and where they had just caught
their splendid butterfly. Europa screamed with
delight; and Phœnix, Cilix, and Cadmus stood
gaping at the spectacle of their sister mounted
on a white bull, not knowing whether to be
frightened or to wish the same good luck for
themselves. The gentle and innocent creature
(for who could possibly doubt that he was so?)
pranced round among the children as sportively
as a kitten. Europa all the while looked down
upon her brothers, nodding and laughing, but yet
with a sort of stateliness in her rosy little face.
As the bull wheeled about to take another gallop
across the meadow, the child waved her hand,
and said, "Good-by," playfully pretending that
she was now bound on a distant journey, and
might not see her brothers again for nobody
could tell how long.

"Good-by," shouted Cadmus, Phœnix, and
Cilix, all in one breath.

But, together with her enjoyment of the sport,
there was still a little remnant of fear in the
child's heart; so that her last look at the three
boys was a troubled one and made them feel as if
their dear sister were really leaving them

"Hercules held him aloft overhead."

"The animal gave a leap up into the air."

forever. And what do you think the snowy bull
did next? Why, he set off as swift as the wind,
straight down to the seashore, scampered across
the sand, took an airy leap, and plunged right in
among the foaming billows. The white spray rose
in a shower over him and little Europa, and fell
spattering down upon the water.

Then what a scream of terror did the poor
child send forth! The three brothers screamed
manfully, likewise, and ran to the shore as fast
as their legs would carry them, with Cadmus at
their head. But it was too late. When they
reached the margin of the sand, the treacherous
animal was already far away in the wide blue
sea, with only his snowy head and tail emerging,
and poor little Europa between them, stretching
out one hand toward her dear brothers, while she
grasped the bull's ivory horn with the other. And
there stood Cadmus, Phœnix, and Cilix, gazing
at this sad spectacle, through their tears, until
they could no longer distinguish the bull's snowy
head from the white-capped billows that seemed
to boil up out of the sea's depths around him.
Nothing more was ever seen of the white bull —
nothing more of the beautiful child.

This was a mournful story, as you may well
think, for the three boys to carry home to their
parents. King Agenor, their father, was the ruler
of the whole country; but he loved his little
daughter Europa better than his kingdom or than
all his other children or than anything else in the
world. Therefore, when Cadmus and his two
brothers came crying home and told him how
that a white bull had carried off their sister and
swam with her over the sea, the king was quite
beside himself with grief and rage. Although it

was now twilight and fast growing dark, he bade
them set out instantly in search of her.

"Never shall you see my face again," he cried,
"unless you bring me back my little Europa, to
gladden me with her smiles and her pretty ways.
Begone, and enter my presence no more, till you
come leading her by the hand."

As King Agenor said this, his eyes flashed fire
(for he was a very passionate king), and he looked
so terribly angry that the poor boys did not even
venture to ask for their suppers, but slunk away
out the the palace and only paused on the steps a
moment to consult whither they should go first.
While they were standing there, all in dismay,
their mother, Queen Telephassa (who happened
not to be by when they told the story to the
king), came hurrying after them and said that she
too would go in quest of her daughter.

"Oh, no, mother!" cried the boys. "The night is
dark and there is no knowing what troubles and
perils we may meet with."

"Alas! my dear children," answered poor Queen
Telephassa, weeping bitterly, "that is only
another reason why I should go with you. If I
should lose you, too, as well as my little Europa,
what would become of me?"

"And let me go likewise"! said their playfellow
Thasus, who came running to join them.

Thasus was the son of a seafaring person in the
neighborhood; he had been brought up with the
young princes, and was their intimate friend and
loved Europa very much; so they consented that
he should accompany them. The whole party,
therefore, set forth together. Cadmus, Phœnix,
Cilix, and Thasus clustered round Queen
Telephassa, grasping her skirts and begging her

to lean upon their shoulders whenever she felt weary. In this manner they went down the palace steps and began a journey which turned out to be a great deal longer than they dreamed of. The last that they saw of King Agenor, he came to the door, with a servant holding a torch beside him, and called after them into the gathering darkness:

"Remember! Never ascent these steps again without the child!"

"Never!" sobbed Queen Telephassa; and the three brothers and Thasus answered, "Never! Never! Never! Never!"

And they kept their word. Year after year King Agenor sat in the solitude of his beautiful palace, listening in vain for their returning footsteps, hoping to hear the familiar voice of the queen and the cheerful talk of his sons and their playfellow Thasus, entering the door together, and the sweet, childish accents of little Europa in the midst of them. But so long a time went by, that, at last, if they had really come, the king would not have known that this was the voice of Telephassa and these the younger voices that used to make such joyful echoes when the children were playing about the palace. We must now leave King Agenor to sit on his throne and must go along with Queen Telephassa and her four youthful companions.

They went on and on, and traveled a long way, passing over mountains and rivers and sailing over seas. Here and there and everywhere, they made continual inquiry if any person could tell them what had become of Europa. The rustic people, of whom they asked this question, paused a little while from their labors in the field and looked very much surprised. They thought it strange to behold a woman in the garb of a queen (for Telephassa, in her haste, had forgotten to take off her crown and her royal robes) roaming about the country, with four lads around her, on such an errand as this seemed to be. But nobody could give them any tidings of Europa; nobody had seen a little girl dressed as a princess and mounted on a snow-white bull, which galloped as swiftly as the wind.

I cannot tell you how long Queen Telephassa and Cadmus, Phœnix, and Cilix, her three sons, and Thasus, their playfellow, went wandering along the highways and by-paths or through the pathless wildernesses of the earth, in this manner. But certain it is, that, before they reached any place of rest, their splendid garments were quite worn out. They all looked very much travel-stained and would have had the dust of many countries on their shoes, if the streams through which they waded had not washed it all away. When they had been gone a year, Telephassa threw away her crown, because it chafed her forehead.

"It has given me many a headache," said the poor queen, "and it cannot cure my heartache."

As fast as their princely robes got torn and tattered, they exchanged them for such mean attire as ordinary people wore. By and by they came to have a wild and homeless aspect; so that you would much sooner have taken them for a gypsy family than a queen and three princes and a young nobleman, who had once a palace for their home and a train of servants to do their bidding. The four boys grew up to be tall young men, with sunburnt faces. Each of them girded on a sword, to defend himself against the perils of the way. When the husband-men, at whose farmhouses they sought hospitality, needed their assistance in the harvest field, they gave it willingly; and Queen Telephassa (who had done no work in her palace, save to braid silk threads with golden ones) came behind them to bind the sheaves. If payment was offered, they shook their heads and only asked for tidings of Europa.

"There are bulls enough in my pasture," the old farmers would reply; "but I never heard of one like this you tell me of. A snow-white bull with a little princess on his back! Ho! ho! I ask your pardon, good folks; but there never was such a sight seen hereabouts."

.At last, when his upper lip began to have the down on it, Phœnix grew weary of rambling hither and thither to no purpose. One day, when they happened to be passing through a pleasant and solitary tract of country, he sat himself down on a heap of moss.

"I can go no farther," said Phœnix. "It is a mere foolish waste of life, to spend it, as we do, in always wandering up and down and never coming to any home at nightfall. Our sister is lost and never will be found. She probably perished in the sea; or, to whatever shore the white bull may have carried her, it is now so many years ago, that there would be neither love nor acquaintance between us, should we meet again. My father has forbidden us to return to his palace; so I shall build me a hut of branches and dwell here."

"Well, son Phœnix," said Telephassa, sorrowfully, "you have grown to be a man and must do as you judge best. But for my part, I will still go in quest of my poor child."

"And we three will go along with you!" cried Cadmus and Cilix and their faithful friend Thasus.

But, before setting out, they all helped Phœnix to build a habitation. When completed, it was a sweet rural bower, roofed overhead with an arch of living boughs. Inside there were two pleasant rooms, one of which had a soft heap of moss for a bed, while the other was furnished with a rustic seat or two, curiously fashioned out of the crooked roots of trees. So comfortable and homelike did it seem that Telephassa and her three companions could not help sighing, to think that they must still roam about the world, instead of spending the remainder of their lives in some such cheerful abode as they had there built for Phœnix. But, when they bade him farewell, Phœnix shed tears and probably regretted that he was no longer to keep them company.

However, he had fixed upon an admirable place to dwell in. And by and by there came other people, who chanced to have no home; and, seeing how pleasant a spot it was, they built themselves huts in the neighborhood of Phœnix's habitation. Thus, before many years went by, a city had grown up there, in the center of which was seen a stately palace of marble, wherein dwelt Phœnix, clothed in a purple robe and wearing a golden crown upon his head. For the inhabitants of the new city, finding that he had royal blood in his veins, had chosen him to be their king. The very first decree of state which King Phœnix issued was, that, if a maiden happened to arrive in the kingdom, mounted on a snow-white bull, and calling herself Europa, his subjects should treat her with the greatest kindness and respect and immediately bring her to the palace. You may see, by this, that Phœnix's conscience never quite ceased to trouble him for giving up the quest of his dear sister and sitting himself down to be comfortable, while his mother and her companions went onward.

But often and often, at the close of a weary day's journey, did Telephassa and Cadmus, Cilix, and Thasus remember the pleasant spot in which they had left Phœnix. It was a sorrowful prospect for these wanderers, that on the morrow they must again set forth, and that, after many nightfalls, they would perhaps be no nearer the close of their toilsome pilgrimage than now. These thoughts made them all melancholy at times, but appeared to torment Cilix more than the rest of the party. At length, one morning, when they were taking their staffs in hand to set out, he thus addressed them:

"My dear mother, and you good brother Cadmus and my friend Thasus, methinks we are like people in a dream. There is no substance in the life which we are leading. It is such a dreary length of time since the white bull carried off my sister Europa that I have quite forgotten how she looked, and the tones of her voice, and, indeed, almost doubt whether such a little girl ever lived in the world. And whether she once lived or no, I am convinced that she no longer survives and that therefore it is the merest folly to waste our own lives and happiness in seeking her. Were we to find her, she would now be a woman grown and would look upon us all as strangers. So, to tell you the truth, I have resolved to take up my abode here; and I entreat you, mother, brother, and friend, to follow my example."

"Not I, for one," said Telephassa; although the poor queen, firmly as she spoke, was so travel-worn that she could hardly put her foot to the ground. "Not I, for one! In the depths of my heart, little Europa is still the rosy child who ran to gather flowers so many years ago. She has not grown to womanhood nor forgotten me. At noon, at night, journeying onward, sitting down to rest, her childish voice is always in my ears, calling, 'Mother! mother!' Stop here who may, there is no repose for me."

"Nor for me," said Cadmus, "while my dear mother pleases to go onward."

And the faithful Thasus, too, was resolved to bear them company. They remained with Cilix a few days, however, and helped him to build a rustic bower, resembling the one which they had formerly built for Phœnix.

When they were bidding him farewell, Cilix burst into tears and told his mother that it seemed just as melancholy a dream to stay there, in solitude, as to go onward. If she really believed that they would ever find Europa, he was willing to continue the search with them, even now. But Telephassa bade him remain there and be happy, if his own heart would let him. So the pilgrims took their leave of him and departed, and were hardly out of sight before some other wandering people came along that way, saw Cilix's habitation, and were greatly delighted with the appearance of the place. There being abundance of unoccupied ground in the neighborhood, these strangers built huts for themselves and were soon joined by a multitude of new settlers, who quickly formed a city. In the middle of it was seen a magnificent palace of colored marble, on the balcony of which, every noontide, appeared Cilix, in a long purple robe, and with a jeweled crown upon his head; for the inhabitants, when they found out that he was a king's son, had considered him the fittest of all men to be a king himself.

One of the first acts of King Cilix's government was to send an expedition, consisting of a grave ambassador and an escort of bold and hardy young men, with orders to visit the principal kingdoms of the earth and inquire whether a young maiden had passed through those regions, galloping swiftly on a white bull. It is, therefore, plain to my mind that Cilix secretly blamed himself for giving up the search for Europa, as long as he was able to put one foot before the other.

As for Telephassa and Cadmus and the good Thasus, it grieves me to think of them, still keeping up that weary pilgrimage. The two young men did their best for the poor queen, helping her over the rough places, often carrying her across rivulets in their faithful arms and seeking to shelter her at nightfall, even when they themselves lay upon the ground. Sad, sad it was to hear them asking of every passer-by if he had seen Europa, so long after the white bull had carried her away. But, though the gray years thrust themselves between and made the child's figure dim in their remembrance, neither of these true-hearted three ever dreamed of giving up the search.

One morning, however, poor Thasus found that he had sprained his ankle, and could not possibly go a step farther.

"After a few days, to be sure," said he, mournfully, "I might make shift to hobble along with a stick but that would only delay you, and perhaps hinder you from finding dear little Europa, after all your pains and trouble. Do go forward, therefore, my beloved companions, and leave me to follow as I may."

"Thou hast been a true friend, dear Thasus," said Queen Telephassa, kissing his forehead. "Being neither my son, nor the brother of our lost Europa, thou hast shown thyself truer to me and her than Phœnix and Cilix did, whom we have left behind us. Without thy loving help, and that of my son Cadmus, my limbs could not have borne me half so far as this. Now, take thy rest, and be at peace. For — and it is the first time I have owned it to myself — I begin to question whether we shall ever find my beloved daughter in this world."

Saying this, the poor queen shed tears, because it was a grievous trial to the mother's heart to confess that her hopes were growing faint. From that day forward, Cadmus noticed that she never traveled with the same alacrity of spirit that had heretofore supported her. Her weight was heavier upon his arm.

Before setting out, Cadmus helped Thasus build a bower; while Telephassa, being too infirm to give any great assistance, advised them how to fit it up and furnish it, so that it might be as comfortable as a hut of branches could. Thasus, however, did not spend all his days in this green bower. For it happened to him, as to Phœnix and Cilix, that other homeless people visited the spot and liked it, and built themselves habitations in the neighborhood. So here, in the course of a few years, was another thriving city with a red freestone palace in the center of it, where Thasus sat upon a throne, doing justice to the people, with a purple robe over his shoulders, a scepter in his hand, and a crown upon his head. The inhabitants had made him king, not for the sake of any royal blood (for none was in his veins), but because Thasus was an upright, true-hearted, and courageous man, and therefore fit to rule.

But, when the affairs of his kingdom were all settled, King Thasus laid aside his purple robe and crown and scepter, and bade his worthiest subject distribute justice to the people in his stead. Then, grasping the pilgrim's staff that had supported him so long, he set forth again, hoping still to discover some hoof mark of the snow-white bull, some trace of the vanished child. He returned, after a lengthened absence, and sat down wearily upon his throne. To his latest hour, nevertheless, King Thasus showed his true-hearted remembrance of Europa, by ordering that a fire should always be kept burning in his palace and a bath steaming hot and food ready to be served up and a bed with snow-white sheets, in case the maiden should arrive and require immediate refreshment. And though Europa never came, the good Thasus had the blessings of many a poor traveler, who profited by the food and lodging which were meant for the little playmate of the king's boyhood.

Telephassa and Cadmus were now pursuing their weary way, with no companion but each other. The queen leaned heavily upon her son's arm, and could walk only a few miles a day. But for all her weakness and weariness, she would not be persuaded to give up the search. It was enough to bring tears into the eyes of bearded men to hear the melancholy tone with which she inquired of every stranger whether he could tell her any news of the lost child.

Have you seen a little girl — no, no, I mean a young maiden of full growth — passing by this way, mounted on a snow-white bull, which gallops as swiftly as the wind?"

"We have seen no such wondrous sight," the people would reply; and very often, taking Cadmus aside, they whispered to him: "Is this stately and sad-looking woman your mother? Surely she is not in her right mind; and you ought to take her home and make her comfortable, and do your best to get this dream out of her fancy."

"It is no dream," said Cadmus. "Everything else is a dream, save that."

But one day, Telephassa seemed feebler than usual, and leaned almost her whole weight on the arm of Cadmus and walked more slowly than ever before. At last they reached a solitary spot, where she told her son that she must needs lie down and take a good, long rest.

"A good, long rest!" she repeated, looking Cadmus tenderly in the face. "A good, long rest, thou dearest one!"

"As long as you please, dear mother," answered Cadmus.

Telephassa bade him sit down on the turf beside her, and then she took his hand.

"My son," said she, fixing her dim eyes most lovingly upon him, "this rest that I speak of will be very long indeed! You must not wait till it is finished. Dear Cadmus, you do not comprehend me. You must make a grave here and lay your mother's weary frame into it. My pilgrimage is over."

Cadmus burst into tears, and for a long time refused to believe that his dear mother was now to be taken from him. But Telephassa reasoned with him and kissed him and at length made him discern that it was better for her spirit to pass away out of the toil, the weariness, the grief and disappointment which had burdened her on earth, ever since the child was lost. He therefore repressed his sorrow and listened to her last words.

"Dearest Cadmus," said she, "thou hast been the truest son that ever mother had and faithful to the very last. Who else would have borne with my infirmities as thou hast! It is owing to thy care, thou tenderest child, that my grave was not dug long years ago, in some valley or on some hillside, that lies far, far behind us. It is enough. Thou shalt wander no more on this hopeless search. But when thou hast laid thy mother in the earth, then go, my son, to Delphi, and inquire of the oracle what thou shalt do next."

"O mother, mother," cried Cadmus, "couldst thou but have seen my sister before this hour!"

"It matters little now," answered Telephassa, and there was a smile upon her face. "I go now to the better world, and sooner or later, shall find my daughter there."

I will not sadden you, my little hearers, with telling how Telephassa died and was buried, but will only say that her dying smile grew brighter, instead of vanishing from her dead face; so that Cadmus felt convinced that, at her very first step into the better world, she had caught Europa in her arms. He planted some flowers on his mother's grave and left them to grow there, to make the place beautiful when he should be far away.

After performing this last sorrowful duty, he set forth alone, and took the road toward the famous oracle of Delphi, as Telephassa had advised him. On his way thither, he still inquired of most people whom he met whether they had seen Europa; for, to say the truth, Cadmus had grown so accustomed to ask the question that it came to his lips as readily as a remark about the weather. He received various answers. Some told him one thing and some another. Among the rest, a mariner affirmed that many years before in a distant country he had heard a rumor about a white bull, which came swimming across the sea with a child on his back, dressed up in flowers that were blighted by the sea water. He did not know what had become of the child or the bull; and Cadmus suspected, indeed, by a queer twinkle in the mariner's eyes, that he was putting a joke upon him and had never really heard anything about the matter.

Poor Cadmus found it more wearisome to travel alone than to bear all his dear mother's weight, while she had kept him company. His heart, you will understand, was now so heavy that it seemed impossible, sometimes, to carry it any farther. But his limbs were strong and active and well accustomed to exercise. He walked swiftly along, thinking of King Agenor and Queen Telephassa and his brothers and the friendly Thasus, all of whom he had left behind him at one point of his pilgrimage or another, and never expected to see them any more. Full of these remembrances, he came within sight of a lofty mountain, which the people thereabouts told him was called Parnassus. On the slope of Mount Parnassus was the famous Delphi, whither Cadmus was going.

This Delphi was supposed to be the very midmost spot of the whole world. The place of the oracle was a certain cavity in the mountain side, over which, when Cadmus came thither, he found a rude bower of branches. It reminded him of those which he had helped to build for Phœnix and Cilix, and afterwards for Thasus. In later times, when multitudes of people came from great distances to put questions to the oracle, a spacious temple of marble was erected over the spot. But in the days of Cadmus, as I have told you, there was only this rustic bower, with its abundance of green foliage and a tuft of shrubbery, that ran wild over the mysterious hole in the hillside.

When Cadmus had thrust a passage through the tangled boughs and made his way into the bower, he did not at first discern the half-hidden cavity. But soon he felt a cold stream of air rushing out of it with so much force that it shook the ringlets on his cheek. Pulling away the shrubbery which clustered over the hole, he bent forward, and spoke in a distinct but reverential tone, as if addressing some unseen personage inside of the mountain.

"Sacred oracle of Delphi," said he, "whither shall I go next in quest of my dear sister Europa?"

There was at first a deep silence and then a rushing sound, or a noise like a long sigh, proceeding out of the interior of the earth. This cavity, you must know, was looked upon as a sort of fountain of truth, which sometimes gushed out in audible words; although, for the most part, these words were such a riddle that they might just as well have stayed at the bottom of the hole. But Cadmus was more fortunate than many others who went to Delphi in search of truth. By and by, the rushing noise began to sound like articulate language. It repeated, over and over again, the following sentence, which, after all, was so like the vague whistle of a blast of air that Cadmus really did not quite know whether it meant anything or not:

"Seek her no more! Seek her no more! Seek her no more!"

"What, then, shall I do?" asked Cadmus.

For, ever since he was a child, you know, it had been the great object of his life to find his sister. From the very hour that he left following the butterfly in the meadow, near his father's palace, he had done his best to follow Europa over land and sea. And now, if he must give up the search, he seemed to have no more business in the world.

But again the sighing gust of air grew into something like a hoarse voice.

"Follow the cow!" it said. "Follow the cow! Follow the cow!"

And when these words had been repeated until Cadmus was tired of hearing them (especially as he could nôt imagine what cow it was, or why he was to follow her), the gusty hold gave vent to another sentence.

"Where the stray cow lies down, there is your home."

These words were pronounced but a single time and died away into a whisper before Cadmus was fully satisfied that he had caught the meaning. He put other questions, but received no answer; only the gust of wind sighed continually out of the cavity and blew the withered leaves rustling along the ground before it.

"Did there really come any words out of the hole," thought Cadmus, "or have I been dreaming all this while?"

He turned away from the oracle and thought himself no wiser than when he came thither. Caring little what might happen to him, he took the first path that offered itself, and went along at a sluggish pace; for, having no object in view nor any reason to go one way more than another, it would certainly have been foolish to make haste. Whenever he met anybody, the old question was at his tongue's end:

"Have you seen a beautiful maiden, dressed like a king's daughter, and mounted on a snow-white bull, that gallops as swiftly as the wind?"

But, remembering what the oracle had said, he only half uttered the words and then mumbled the rest indistinctly; and from his confusion, people must have imagined that this handsome young man had lost his wits.

I know not how far Cadmus had gone nor could he himself have told you, when, at no great distance before him, he beheld a brindled cow. She was lying down by the wayside and quietly chewing her cud; nor did she take any notice of the young man until he had approached pretty nigh. Then, getting leisurely upon her feet and giving her head a gentle toss, she began to move along at a moderate pace, often pausing just long enough to crop a mouthful of grass. Cadmus loitered behind, whistling idly to himself and scarcely noticing the cow; until the thought occurred to him, whether this could possibly be the animal which, according to the oracle's response, was to serve him for a guide. But he smiled at himself for fancying such a thing. He could not seriously think that this was the cow, because she went along so quietly, behaving just like any other cow. Evidently she neither knew nor cared so much as a wisp of hay about Cadmus and was only thinking how to get her living along the wayside, where the herbage was green and fresh. Perhaps she was going home to be milked.

"Cow, cow, cow!" cried Cadmus. "Hey, Brindle, hey! Stop, my good cow."

He wanted to come up with the cow, so as to examine her and see if she would appear to know him or whether there were any peculiarities to distinguish her from a thousand other cows, whose only business is to fill the milk pail, and sometimes kick it over. But still the brindled cow trudged on, whisking her tail to keep the flies away, and taking as little notice of Cadmus as she well could. If he walked slowly, so did the cow, and seized the opportunity to graze. If he quickened his pace, the cow went just so much the faster; and once, when Cadmus tried to catch her by running, she threw out her heels, stuck her tail straight on end, and set off at a gallop, looking as queerly as cows generally do while putting themselves to their speed.

When Cadmus saw that it was impossible to come up with her, he walked on moderately as before. The cow, too, went leisurely on, without looking behind. Wherever the grass was greenest, there she nibbled a mouthful or two. Where a brook glistened brightly across the path, there the cow drank and breathed a comfortable sigh, and drank again and trudged onward at the pace that best suited herself and Cadmus.

"I do believe," thought Cadmus, "that this may be the cow that was foretold me. If it be the one, I suppose she will lie down somewhere hereabouts."

Whether it were the oracular cow or some other one, it did not seem reasonable that she should travel a great way farther. So, whenever they reached a particularly pleasant spot on a breezy hillside or in a sheltered vale or flowery meadow, on the shore of a calm lake or along the bank of a clear stream, Cadmus looked eagerly around to see if the situation would suit him for a home. But still, whether he liked the place or no, the brindled cow never offered to lie down. On she went at the quiet pace of a cow going homeward to the barnyard; and, every moment, Cadmus expected to see a milkmaid approaching with a pail, or a herdsman running to head the stray animal and turn her back toward the pasture. But no milkmaid came; no herdsman drove her back; and Cadmus followed the stray Brindle till he was almost ready to drop down with fatigue.

"O brindled cow," cried he, in a tone of despair, "do you never mean to stop?"

He had now grown too intent on following her to think of lagging behind, however long the way and whatever might be his fatigue. Indeed, it seemed as if there were something about the animal that bewitched people. Several persons who happened to see the brindled cow and Cadmus following behind, began to trudge after her, precisely as he did. Cadmus was glad of somebody to converse with, and therefore talked very freely to these good people. He told them all his adventures, and how he had left King Agenor in his palace, and Phœnix at one place and Cilix at another and Thasus at a third and his dear mother, Queen Telephassa, under a flowery sod; so that now he was quite alone, both friendless and homeless. He mentioned, likewise, that the oracle had bidden him be guided by a cow, and inquired of the strangers whether they supposed that this brindled animal could be the one.

"Why, 'tis a very wonderful affair," answered one of his new companions. "I am pretty well acquainted with the ways of cattle, and I never knew a cow, of her own accord, to go so far without stopping. If my legs will let me, I'll never leave following the beast till she lies down."

"Nor I!" said a second.

"Nor I!" cried a third. "If she goes a hundred miles farther, I'm determined to see the end of it."

The secret of it was, you must know, that the cow was an enchanted cow, and that, without their being conscious of it, she threw some of her enchantment over everybody that took so much as half a dozen steps behind her. They could not possibly help following her, though all the time they fancied themselves doing it of their own accord. The cow was by no means very nice in choosing her path; sometimes they had to scramble over rocks or wade through mud and mire, and were all in a terribly bedraggled condition and tired to death and very hungry, into the bargain. What a weary business it was!

But still they kept trudging stoutly forward and talking as they went. The strangers grew very fond of Cadmus, and resolved never to leave him, but to help him build a city wherever the cow might lie down. In the center of it there should be a noble palace, in which Cadmus might dwell and be their king, with a throne, a crown, and scepter, a purple robe, and everything else that a king ought to have; for in him there was the royal blood and the royal heart and the head that knew how to rule.

While they were talking of these schemes and beguiling the tediousness of the way with laying out the plan of the new city, one of the company happened to look at the cow.

"Joy! joy!" cried he, clapping his hands. "Brindle is going to lie down."

They all looked; and, sure enough, the cow had stopped, and was staring leisurely about her, as other cows do when on the point of lying down. And slowly, slowly did she recline herself on the soft grass, first bending her forelegs and then crouching her hind ones. When Cadmus and his companions came up with her, there was the brindled cow taking her ease, chewing her cud, and looking them quietly in the face; as if this was just the spot she had been seeking for and as if it were all a matter of course.

"This, then," said Cadmus, gazing around him, "this is to be my home."

It was a fertile and lovely plain, with great trees flinging their sun-speckled shadows over it and hills fencing it in from the rough weather. At no great distance, they beheld a river gleaming in the sunshine. A home feeling stole into the heart of poor Cadmus. He was very glad to know that here he might awake in the morning, without the necessity of putting on his dusty sandals to travel farther and farther. The days and the years would pass over him and find him still in this pleasant spot. If he could have had his brothers with him and his friend Thasus, and could have seen his dear mother under a roof of his own, he might here have been happy, after all their disappointments. Some day or other, too his sister Europa might have come quietly to the door of his home and smiled round upon the familiar faces. But, indeed, since there was no hope of regaining the friends of his boyhood or ever seeking his dear sister again, Cadmus resolved to make himself happy with these new companions, who had grown so fond of him while following the cow.

"Yes, my friends," said he to them, "this is to be our home. Here we will build our habitations. The brindled cow, which has led us hither, will supply us with milk. We will cultivate the neighboring soil and lead an innocent and happy life."

His companions joyfully assented to this plan; and, in the first place, being very hungry and thirsty, they looked about them for the means of providing a comfortable meal. Not far off, they saw a tuft of trees, which appeared as if there might be a spring of water beneath them. They went thither to fetch some, leaving Cadmus stretched on the ground along with the brindled cow; for, now that he had found a place of rest, it seemed as if all the weariness of his pilgrimage ever since he left King Agenor's palace, had fallen upon him at once. But his new friends had not long been gone, when he was suddenly startled by cries, shouts, and screams, and the noise of a terrible struggle, and in the midst of it all, a most awful hissing, which went right through his ears like a rough saw.

Running toward the tuft of trees, he beheld the head and firery eyes of an immense serpent or dragon, with the widest jaws that ever a dragon had, and a vast many rows of horribly sharp teeth. Before Cadmus could reach the spot, this pitiless reptile had killed his poor companions, and was busy devouring them, making but a mouthful of each man.

It appears that the fountain of water was enchanted and that the dragon had been set to guard it, so that no mortal might ever quench his thirst there. As the neighboring inhabitants carefully avoided the spot, it was now a long time (not less than a hundred years, or thereabouts) since the monster had broken his fast; and, as was natural enough, his appetite had grown to be enormous and was not half satisfied by the poor people whom he had just eaten up. When he caught sight of Cadmus, therefore, he set up another abominable hiss and flung back his immense jaws, until his mouth looked like a great red cavern, at the farther end of which were seen the legs of his last victim, whom he had hardly had time to swallow.

But Cadmus was so enraged at the destruction of his friends that he cared neither for the size of the dragon's jaws nor for his hundreds of sharp teeth. Drawing his sword, he rushed at the monster and

flung himself right into his cavernous mouth. This
bold method of attacking him took the dragon by
surprise; for, in fact, Cadmus had leaped so far
down into his throat that the rows of terrible teeth
could not close upon him, nor do him the least harm
in the world. Thus, though the struggle was a
tremendous one, and though the dragon shattered
the tuft of trees into small splinters by the lashing
of his tail, yet, as Cadmus was all the while slashing
and stabbing at his very vitals, it was not long
before the scaly wretch bethought himself of
slipping away. He had not gone his length, however,
when the brave Cadmus gave him a sword thrust
that finished the battle; and, creeping out of the
gateway of the creature's jaws, there he beheld him
still wriggling his vast bulk, although there was no
longer life enough in him to harm a little child.

But do not you suppose that it made Cadmus
sorrowful to think of the melancholy fate which had
befallen those poor, friendly people, who had
followed the cow along with him? It seemed as if he
were doomed to lose everybody whom he loved or to
see them perish in one way or another. And here he
was, after all his toils and troubles, in a solitary
place, with not a single human being to help him
build a hut.

"What shall I do?" cried he aloud. "It were better
for me to have been devoured by the dragon, as my
poor companions were."

"Cadmus," said a voice — but whether it came
from above or below him, or whether it spoke within
his own breast, the young man could not tell —
"Cadmus, pluck out the dragon's teeth, and plant
them in the earth."

This was a strange thing to do; nor was it very
easy, I should imagine, to dig out all those deep-

rooted fangs from the dead dragon's jaws. But Cadmus toiled and tugged, and after pounding the monstrous head almost to pieces with a great stone, he at last collected as many teeth as might have filled a bushel or two. The next thing was to plant them. This, likewise, was a tedious piece of work, especially as Cadmus was already exhausted with killing the dragon and knocking his head to pieces, and had nothing to dig the earth with, that I know of, unless it were his sword blade. Finally, however, a sufficiently large tract of ground was turned up and sown with this new kind of seed; although half of the dragon's teeth still remained to be planted some other day.

Cadmus, quite out of breath, stood leaning upon his sword and wondering what was to happen next. He had waited but a few moments, when he began to see a sight, which was as great a marvel as the most marvelous thing I ever told you about.

The sun was shining slantwise over the field, and showed all the moist, dark soil, just like any other newly planted piece of ground. All at once, Cadmus fancied he saw something glisten very brightly, first at one spot, then at another, and then at a hundred and a thousand spots together. Soon he perceived them to be the steel heads of spears, sprouting up everywhere like so many stalks of grain and continually growing taller and taller. Next appeared a vast number of bright sword blades, thrusting themselves up in the same way. A moment afterwards, the whole surface of the ground was broken by a multitude of polished brass helmets, coming up like a crop of enormous beans. So rapidly did they grow that Cadmus now discerned the fierce countenance of a man beneath every one. In short, before he had time to think what a wonderful affair it was, he beheld an abundant harvest of what looked like human beings, armed with helmets and breastplates, shields, swords, and spears; and before they were well out of the earth, they brandished their weapons and clashed them one against another, seeming to think, little while as they had yet lived, that they had wasted too much of life without a battle. Every tooth of the dragon had reproduced one of these sons of deadly mischief.

Up sprouted, also, a great many trumpeters; and with the first breath that they drew they put their brazen trumpets to their lips and sounded a tremendous and ear-shattering blast; so that the whole space, just now so quiet and solitary, reverberated with the clash and clang of arms, the bray of warlike music, and the shouts of angry men. So enraged did they all look that Cadmus fully expected them to put the whole world to the sword. How fortunate would it be for a great conqueror, if he could get a bushel of the dragon's teeth to sow!

"Cadmus," said the same voice which he had before heard, "throw a stone into the midst of the armed men."

So Cadmus seized a large stone, and, flinging it into the middle of the earth army, saw it strike the breastplate of a gigantic and fierce-looking warrior. Immediately on feeling the blow, he seemed to take it for granted that somebody had struck him; and, uplifting his weapon, he smote his next neighbor a blow that cleft his helmet asunder and stretched him on the ground. In an instant those nearest the fallen

warrior began to strike at one another with their
swords and stab with their spears. The confusion
spread wider and wider. Each man smote down
his brother and was himself smitten down before
he' had time to exult in his victory. The
trumpeters, all the while, blew their blasts
shriller and shriller; each soldier shouted a battle
cry and often fell with it on his lips. It was the
strangest spectacle of causeless wrath and of
mischief for no good end, that had ever been
witnessed; but, after all, it was neither more
foolish nor more wicked than a thousand battles
that have since been fought, in which men have
slain their brothers with just as little reason as
these children of the dragon's teeth. It ought to
be considered, too, that the dragon people were
made for nothing else; whereas other mortals
were born to love and help one another.

Well, this memorable battle continued to rage
until the ground was strewn with helmeted heads
that had been cut off. Of all the thousands that
began the fight, there were only five left
standing. These now rushed from different parts
of the field, and, meeting in the middle of it,
clashed their swords and struck at each other's
hearts as fiercely as ever.

"Cadmus," said the voice again, "bid those five
warriors sheathe their swords. They will help
you to build the city."

Without hesitating an instant, Cadmus stepped
forward, with the aspect of a king and a leader
and extending his drawn sword amongst them,
spoke to the warriors in a stern and commanding
voice.

"Sheathe your weapons!" said he.

Forthwith, feeling themselves bound to obey

him, the five remaining sons of the dragon's teeth made him a military salute with their swords, returned them to the scabbards, and stood before Cadmus in a rank, eyeing him as soldiers eye their captain, while awaiting the word of command.

These five men had probably sprung from the biggest of the dragon's teeth and were the boldest and strongest of the whole army. They were almost giants, indeed, and had good need to be so, else they never could have lived through so terrible a fight. They still had a very furious look, and, if Cadmus happened to glance aside, would glare at one another, with fire flashing out of their eyes. It was strange, too, to observe how the earth, out of which they had so lately grown, was incrusted, here and there, on their bright breastplates, and even begrimed their faces, just as you may have seen it clinging to beets and carrots when pulled out of their native soil. Cadmus hardly knew whether to consider them as men, or some odd kind of vegetable; although, on the whole, he concluded that there was human nature in them, because they were so fond of trumpets and weapons and so ready to shed blood.

They looked him earnestly in the face, waiting for his next order, and evidently desiring no other employment than to follow him from one battle field to another, all over the wide world. But Cadmus was wiser than these earthborn creatures, with the dragon's fierceness in them, and knew better how to use their strength and hardihood.

"Come!" said he. "You are sturdy fellows. Make yourselves useful! Quarry some stones with those great swords of yours and help me to build a city."

The five soldiers grumbled a little and muttered that it was their business to overthrow cities, not to build them up. But Cadmus looked at them with a stern eye and spoke to them in a tone of authority, so that they knew him for their master and never again thought of disobeying his commands. They set to work in good earnest and toiled so diligently, that in a very short time, a city began to make its appearance. At first, to be sure, the workmen showed a quarrelsome disposition. Like savage beasts, they would doubtless have done one another a mischief, if Cadmus had not kept watch over them and quelled the fierce old serpent that lurked in their hearts when he saw it gleaming out of their wild eyes. But, in course of time, they got accustomed to honest labor, and had sense enough to feel that there was more true enjoyment in living at peace and doing good to one's neighbor, than in striking at him with a two-edge sword. It may not be too much to hope that the rest of mankind will by and by grow as wise and peaceable as these five earth-begrimed warriors, who sprang from the dragon's teeth.

And now the city was built, and there was a home in it for each of the workmen. But the palace of Cadmus was not yet erected, because they had left it till the last, meaning to introduce all the new improvements of architecture and make it very commodious, as well as stately and beautiful. After finishing the rest of their labors, they all went to bed betimes, in order to rise in the gray of the morning, and to get at least the foundation of the edifice laid before nightfall. But, when Cadmus arose, and took his way toward the site where the palace was to be built, followed by his five sturdy workmen marching all in a row, what do you think he saw?

What should it be but the most magnificent palace that had ever been seen in the world! It was built of marble and other beautiful kinds of stone, and rose high into the air, with a splendid dome and a portico along the front, and carved pillars and everything else that befitted the habitation of a mighty king. It had grown up out of the earth in almost as short a time as it had taken the armed host to spring from the dragon's teeth; and what made the matter more strange, no seed of this stately edifice had ever been planted.

When the five workmen beheld the dome, with the morning sunshine making it look golden and glorious, they gave a great shout.

"Long live King Cadmus," they cried, "in his beautiful palace!"

And the new king, with his five faithful followers at his heels, shouldering their pickaxes and marching in a rank (for they still had a soldier-like sort of behavior, as their nature was), ascended the palace steps. Halting at the entrance, they gazed through a long vista of lofty pillars that were ranged from end to end of a great hall. At the farther extremity of this hall, approaching slowly toward him, Cadmus beheld a female figure, wonderfully beautiful, and adorned with a royal robe and a crown of diamonds over her golden ringlets, and the richest necklace that ever a queen wore. His heart thrilled with delight. He fancied it his long-lost sister Europa, now grown to woman-hood, coming to make him happy, and to repay him with her sweet and sisterly affection, for all those weary wanderings in quest of her since he left King Agenor's palace — for the tears that he had shed, on parting with Phœnix and Cilix and Thasus — for the heartbreakings that had made the whole world seem dismal to him over his dear mother's grave.

But, as Cadmus advanced to meet the beautiful stranger, he saw that her features were unknown to him, although, in the little time that it required to tread along the hall, he had already felt a sympathy betwixt himself and her.

"No, Cadmus," said the same voice that had spoken to him in the field of the armed men, "this is not that dear sister Europa whom you have sought so faithfully all over the wide world. This is Harmonia, a daughter of the sky, who is given you instead of sister and brothers and friend and mother. You will find all those dear ones in her alone."

So King Cadmus dwelt in the palace, with his new friend Harmonia, and found a great deal of comfort in his magnificent abode, but would doubtless have found as much, if not more, in the humblest cottage by the wayside. Before many years went by, there was a group of rosy little children (but how they came thither has always been a mystery to me) sporting in the great hall and on the marble steps of the palace and running joyfully to meet King Cadmus when affairs of state left him at leisure to play with them. They called him father, and Queen Harmonia mother. The five old soldiers of the dragon's teeth grew very fond of these small urchins, and were never weary of showing them how to shoulder sticks, flourish wooden swords, and march in military order, blowing a penny trumpet or beating an abominable rub-a-dub upon a little drum.

But King Cadmus, lest there should be too much of the dragon's tooth in his children's disposition, used to find time from his kingly duties to teach them their A B C — which he invented for their benefit, and for which many little people, I am afraid, are not half so grateful to him as they ought to be.

Circe's Palace

SOME of you have heard, no doubt, of the wise King Ulysses and how he went to the siege of Troy, and how, after that famous city was taken and burned, he spent ten long years in trying to get back again to his own little kingdom of Ithaca. At one time in the course of this weary voyage, he arrived at an island that looked very green and pleasant, but the name of which was unknown to him. Only a little while before he came thither, he had met with a terrible hurricane, or rather a great many hurricanes at once, which drove his fleet of vessels into a strange part of the sea, where neither himself nor any of his mariners had ever sailed. This misfortune was entirely owing to the foolish curiosity of his shipmates, who, while Ulysses lay asleep, had untied some very bulky leathern bags, in which they supposed a valuable treasure to be concealed. But in each of these stout bags, King AEolus, the ruler of the winds, had tied up a tempest and had given it to Ulysses to keep, in order that he might be sure of a favorable passage homeward to Ithaca. When the strings were loosened, forth rushed the whistling blasts, like air out of a blown bladder, whitening the sea with foam and scattering the vessels nobody could tell whither.

Immediately after escaping from this peril, a still greater one had befallen him. Scudding before the hurricane, he reached a place, which, as he afterwards found was called Læstrygonia, where some monstrous giants had eaten up many of his companions and had sunk every one of his vessels, except that in which he himself sailed, by flinging great masses of rock at them from the cliffs along the shore. After going through such troubles as these, you cannot wonder that King Ulysses was glad to moor his tempest-beaten bark in a quiet cove of the green island, which I began with telling you about. But he had encountered so many dangers from giants and one-eyed Cyclopes and monsters of the sea and land, that he could not help dreading some mischief, even in this pleasant and seemingly solitary spot. For two days, therefore, the poor weather-worn voyagers kept quiet, and either stayed on board of their vessel or merely crept along under the cliffs that bordered the shore. To keep themselves alive, they dug shellfish out of the sand and sought for any little rill of fresh water that might be running toward the sea.

Before the two days were spent, they grew very weary of this kind of life; for the followers of King Ulysses, as you will find it important to remember, were terrible gormandizers, and pretty sure to grumble if they missed their regular meals and their irregular ones besides. Their stock of provisions was quite exhausted, and even the shellfish began to get scarce, so that they had now to choose between starving to death or venturing into the interior of the island, where perhaps some huge three-headed dragon, or other horrible monster, had his den. Such misshapen creatures were very numerous in those days; and nobody ever expected to make a voyage, or take a journey, without running more or less risk of being devoured by them.

But King Ulysses was a bold man as well as a prudent one. On the third morning he determined to discover what sort of place the island was and whether it were possible to obtain a supply of food for the hungry mouths of his companions. Taking a spear in his hand, he clambered to the summit of a cliff, and gazed round about him. At a distance, toward the center of the island, he beheld the stately towers of what seemed to be a palace, built of snow-white marble and rising in the midst of a grove of lofty trees.

The thick branches of these trees stretched across the front of the edifice and more than half concealed it, although, from the portion which he saw, Ulysses judged it to be spacious and exceedingly beautiful, and probably the residence of some great nobleman or prince. A blue smoke went curling up from the chimney and was almost the pleasantest part of the spectacle to Ulysses. For, from the abundance of this smoke, it was reasonable to conclude that there was a good fire in the kitchen, and that, at dinner time, a plentiful banquet would be served up to the inhabitants of the palace and to whatever guests might happen to drop in.

With so agreeable a prospect before him,

Ulysses fancied that he could not do better than to go straight to the palace gate and tell the master of it that there was a crew of poor shipwrecked mariners not far off, who had eaten nothing for a day or two save a few clams and oysters and would therefore be thankful for a little food. And the prince or nobleman must be a very stingy curmudgeon, to be sure, if, at least, when his own dinner was over, he would not bid them welcome to the broken victuals from the table.

Pleasing himself with this idea, King Ulysses had made a few steps in the direction of the palace, when there was a great twittering and chirping from the branch of a neighboring tree. A moment afterwards, a bird came flying toward him and hovered in the air, so as almost to brush his face with its wings. It was a very pretty little bird, with purple wings and body and yellow legs, and a circle of golden feathers round its neck and on its head a golden tuft, which looked like a king's crown in miniature. Ulysses tried to catch the bird. But it fluttered nimbly out of his reach, still chirping in a piteous tone, as if it could have told a lamentable story, had it only been gifted with human language. When he attempted to drive it away, the bird flew no farther than the bough of the next tree and again came fluttering about his head, with its doleful chirp, as soon as he showed a purpose of going forward.

"Have you anything to tell me, little bird?" asked Ulysses.

He was ready to listen attentively to whatever the bird might communicate; for at the siege of Troy and elsewhere, he had known such odd things to happen, that he would not have considered it much out of the common run had this little feathered creature talked as plainly as himself.

"Peep!" said the bird, "peep, peep, pe — weep!" and nothing else would it say, but only, "Peep, peep, pe — weep!" in a melancholy cadence, and over and over and over again. As often as Ulysses moved forward, however, the bird showed the greatest alarm and did its best to drive him back, with the anxious flutter of its purple wings. Its unaccountable behavior made him conclude, at last, that the bird knew of some danger that awaited him and which must needs be very terrible, beyond all question, since it moved even a little fowl to feel compassion for a human being. He resolved, for the present, to return to the vessel and tell his companions what he had seen.

This appeared to satisfy the bird. As soon as Ulysses turned back, it ran up the trunk of a tree and began to pick insects out of the bark with its long, sharp bill; it was a kind of woodpecker, you must know, and had to get its living in the same manner as other birds of that species. But every little while, as it pecked at the bark of the tree, the purple bird bethought itself of some secret sorrow, and repeated its plaintive note of "Peep, peep, pe — weep!"

On his way to the shore, Ulysses had the good luck to kill a large stag by thrusting his spear into its back. Taking it on his shoulders (for he was a remarkably strong man), he lugged it along with him and flung it down before his hungry companions. I have already hinted to you what gormandizers some of the comrades of King

Ulysses were. From what is related of them, I
reckon that their favorite diet was pork, and that
they had lived upon it until a good part of their
physical substance was swine's flesh and their
tempers and dispositions were very much akin to
the hog. A dish of venison, however, was no
unacceptable meal to them, especially after
feeding so long on oysters and clams. Beholding
the dead stag, they felt of its ribs, in a knowing
way, and lost no time in kindling a fire of
driftwood to cook it. The rest of the day was
spent in feasting; and if these enormous eaters
got up from the table at sunset, it was only
because they could not scrape another morsel off
the poor animal's bones.

The next morning their appetites were as sharp
as ever. They looked at Ulysses, as if they
expected him to clamber up the cliff again and
come back with another fat deer upon his
shoulders. Instead of setting out, however, he
summoned the whole crew together and told
them it was in vain to hope that he could kill a
stag every day for their dinner, and therefore it
was advisable to think of some other mode of
satisfying their hunger.

"Now," said he, "when I was on the cliff
yesterday, I discovered that this island is
inhabited. At a considerable distance from the
shore stood a marble palace, which appeared to
be very spacious and had a great deal of smoke
curling out of one of its chimneys."

"Aha!" muttered some of his companions,
smacking their lips. "That smoke must have
come from the kitchen fire. There was a good
dinner on the spit; and no doubt there will be as
good a one today."

"But," continued the wise Ulysses, "you must remember, my good friends, our misadventure in the cavern of one-eyed Polyphemus, the Cyclops! Instead of his ordinary milk diet, did he not eat up two of our comrades for his supper and a couple more for breakfast and two at his supper again? Methinks I see him yet, the hideous monster, scanning us with that great red eye, in the middle of his forehead, to single out the fattest. And then, again, only a few days ago, did we not fall into the hands of this king of the Læstrygones, and those other horrible giants, his subjects, who devoured a great many more of us than are now left? To tell you the truth, if we go to yonder palace, there can be no question that we shall make our appearance at the dinner table; but whether seated as guests or served up as food, is a point to be seriously considered."

"Either way," murmured some of the hungriest of the crew, "it will be better than starvation; particularly if one could be sure of being well fattened beforehand and daintly cooked afterwards."

"That is a matter of taste," said King Ulysses, "and, for my own part, neither the most careful fattening nor the daintiest of cookery would reconcile me to being dished at last. My proposal is, therefore, that we divide ourselves into two equal parties and ascertain, by drawing lots, which of the two shall go to the palace and beg for food and assistance. If these can be obtained, all is well. If not, and if the inhabitants prove as inhospitable as Polyphemus, or the Læstrygones, then there will but half of us perish and the remainder may set sail and escape."

As nobody objected to this scheme, Ulysses proceeded to count the whole band and found that there were forty-six men including himself. He then numbered off twenty-two of them and put Eurylochus (who was one of his chief officers, and second only to himself in sagacity) at their head. Ulysses took command of the remaining twenty-two men, in person. Then, taking off his helmet, he put two shells into it, on one of which was written, "Go," and on the other "Stay." Another person now held the helmet, while Ulysses and Eurylochus drew out each a shell; and the word "Go" was found written on that which Eurylochus had drawn. In this manner, it was decided that Ulysses and his twenty-two men were to remain at the seaside until the other party should have found out what sort of treatment they might expect at the mysterious palace. As there was no help for it, Eurylochus immediately set forth at the head of his twenty-two followers, who went off in a very melancholy state of mind, leaving their friends in hardly better spirits than themselves.

No sooner had they clambered up the cliff than they discerned the tall marble towers of the palace, ascending, as white as snow, out of the lovely green shadow of the trees which surrounded it. A gush of smoke came from a chimney in the rear of the edifice. This vapor rose high in the air, and, meeting with a breeze, was wafted seaward and made to pass over the heads of the hungry mariners. When people's appetites are keen, they have a very quick scent for anything savory in the wind.

"That smoke comes from the kitchen!" cried one of them, turning up his nose as high as he could and snuffing eagerly. "And, as sure as I'm a half-starved vagabond, I smell roast meat in it."

"Pig, roast pig!" said another. "Ah, the dainty little porker! My mouth waters for him."

"Let us make haste," cried the others, "or we shall be too late for the good cheer!"

But scarcely had they made half a dozen steps from the edge of the cliff, when a bird came fluttering to meet them. It was the same pretty little bird, with the purple wings and body, the yellow legs, the golden collar round its neck, and the crownlike tuft upon its head, whose behavior had so much surprised Ulysses. It hovered about Eurylochus and almost brushed his face with its wings.

"Peep, peep, pe — weep!" chirped the bird.

So plaintively intelligent was the sound that it seemed as if the little creature were going to break its heart with some mighty secret that it had to tell, and only this one poor note to tell it with.

"My pretty bird," said Eurylochus — for he was a wary person and let no token of harm escape his notice — "my pretty bird, who sent you hither? And what is the message which you bring?"

"Peep, peep, pe — weep!" replied the bird, very sorrowfully.

Then it flew toward the edge of the cliff and looked around at them, as if exceedingly anxious that they should return whence they came. Eurylochus and a few of the others were inclined to turn back. They could not help suspecting that the purple bird must be aware of something mischievous that would befall them at the palace, the knowledge of which affected its airy spirit with a human sympathy and sorrow. But the rest of the voyagers, snuffing up the smoke from the palace kitchen, ridiculed the idea of returning to the vessel. One of them (more brutal than his fellows, and the most notorious gormandizer in the whole crew) said such a cruel and wicked thing, that I wonder the mere thought did not turn him into a wild beast, in shape, as he already was in his nature.

"This troublesome and impertinent little fowl," said he, "would make a delicate tidbit to begin dinner with. Just one plump morsel, melting away between the teeth. If he comes within my reach, I'll catch him and give him to the palace cook to be roasted on a skewer."

The words were hardly out of his mouth, before the purple bird flew away, crying, "Peep, peep, pe — weep," more dolorously than ever.

"That bird," remarked Eurylochus, "knows more than we do about what awaits us at the palace."

"Come on, then," cried his comrades, "and we'll soon know as much as he does."

The party, accordingly, went onward through the green and pleasant wood. Every little while they caught new glimpses of the marble palace, which looked more and more beautiful the nearer they approached it. They soon entered a broad pathway which seemed to be very neatly kept and which went winding along with streaks of sunshine falling across it and specks of light quivering among the deepest shadows that fell from the lofty trees. It was bordered, too, with a great many sweet-smelling flowers such as the mariners had never seen before. So rich and beautiful were they, that, if the shrubs grew wild here, and were native in the soil, then this island was surely the flower garden of the whole earth; or, if transplanted from some other clime, it must have been from the Happy Islands that lay toward the golden sunset.

"There has been a great deal of pains foolishly wasted on these flowers," observed one of the company; and I tell you what he said, that you may keep in mind what gormandizers they were. "For my part, if I were the owner of the palace, I would bid my gardener cultivate nothing buy savory potherbs to make a stuffing for roast meat, or to flavor a stew with."

"Well said!" cried the others. "But I'll warrant you there's a kitchen garden in the rear of the palace."

At one place they came to a crystal spring and paused to drink at it for want of liquor which they liked better. Looking into its bosom, they beheld their own faces dimly reflected, but so extravagantly distorted by the gush and motion of the water, that each one of them appeared to be laughing at himself and all his companions. So ridiculous were these images of themselves, indeed, that they did really laugh aloud, and could hardly be grave again as soon as they wished. And after they had drunk, they grew still merrier than before.

"It has a twang of the wine cask in it," said one, smacking his lips.

"Make haste!" cried his fellows: "we'll find the wine cask itself at the palace. That will be better than a hundred crystal fountains."

Then they quickened their pace and capered for joy at the thought of the savory banquet at which they hoped to be guests. But Eurylochus told them that he felt as if he were walking in a dream.

"If I am really awake," continued he, "then, in my opinion, we are on the point of meeting with some stranger adventure than any that befell us in the cave of Polyphemus, or among the gigantic man-eating Læstrygones, or in the windy palace of King Æolus, which stands on a brazen-walled island. This kind of dreamy feeling always comes over me before any wonderful occurrence. If you take my advice, you will turn back."

"No, no," answered his comrades, snuffing the air, in which the scent from the palace kitchen was now very perceptible. "We would not turn back, though we were certain that the king of the Læstrygones, as big as a mountain, would sit at the head of the table, and huge Polyphemus, the one-eyed Cyclops, at its foot."

At length they came within full sight of the palace, which proved to be very large and lofty, with a great number of airy pinnacles upon its roof. Though it was now midday and the sun shone brightly over the marble front, yet its snowy whiteness and its fantastic style of architecture made it look unreal, like the frostwork on a windowpane, or like the shapes of castles which one sees among the clouds by moonlight. But just then, a puff of wind brought down the smoke of the kitchen chimney among them, and caused each man to smell the odor of the dish that he liked best; after scenting it, they thought everything else moonshine and nothing real save this palace, and save the banquet that was evidently ready to be served up in it.

They hastened their steps toward the portal,

but had not got halfway across the wide lawn, when a pack of lions, tigers, and wolves came bounding to meet them. The terrified mariners, started back, expecting no better fate than to be torn to pieces and devoured. To their surprise and joy, however, these wild beasts merely capered around them, wagging their tails, offering their heads to be stroked and patted and behaving just like so many well-bred house dogs, when they wish to express their delight at meeting their master or their master's friends. They biggest lion licked the feet of Eurylochus; and every other lion and every wolf and tiger singled out one of his two and twenty followers, whom the beast fondled as if he loved him better than a beef bone.

But for all that, Eurylochus imagined that he saw something fierce and savage in their eyes; nor would he have been surprised, at any moment, to feel the big lion's terrible claws or to see each of the tigers make a deadly spring, or each wolf leap at the throat of the man whom he had fondled. Their mildness seemed unreal and a mere freak; but their savage nature was as true as their teeth and claws.

Nevertheless, the men went safely across the lawn with the wild beasts frisking about them and doing no manner of harm; although, as they mounted the steps of the palace, you might possibly have heard a low growl, particularly from the wolves; as if they thought it a pity, after all, to let the strangers pass without so much as tasting what they were made of.

Eurylochus and his followers now passed under a lofty portal and looked through the open doorway into the interior of the palace. The first thing that they saw was a spacious hall and a fountain in the middle of it, gushing up toward the ceiling out of a marble basin and falling back into it with a continual splash. The water of this fountain, as it spouted upward, was constantly taking new shapes, not very distinctly, but plainly enough for a nimble fancy to recognize what they were. Now it was the shape of a man in a long robe, the fleecy whiteness of which was made out of the fountain's spray; now it was a lion or a tiger or a wolf or an ass, or, as often as anything else, a hog, wallowing in the marble basin as if it were his sty. It was either magic or some very curious machinery that caused the gushing waterspout to assume all these forms. But, before the strangers had time to look closely at this wonderful sight, their attention was drawn off by a very sweet and agreeable sound. A woman's voice was singing melodiously in another room of the palace, and with her voice was mingled the noise of a loom, at which she was probably seated, weaving a rich texture of cloth, and intertwinging the high and low sweetness of her voice into a rich tissue of harmony.

By and by, the song came to an end; and then, all at once, there were several feminine voices, talking airily and cheerfully, with now and then a merry burst of laughter, such as you may always hear when three or four young women sit at work together.

"What a sweet song that was!" exclaimed one of the voyagers.

"Too sweet, indeed," answered Eurylochus, shaking his head. "Yet it was not so sweet as the song of the Sirens, those birdlike damsels who wanted to tempt us on the rocks, so that our vessel might be wrecked and our bones left whitening along the shore."

"But just listen to the pleasant voices of those maidens, and that buzz of the loom as the shuttle passes to and fro," said another comrade. "What a domestic, household, homelike sound it is! Ah, before that weary siege of Troy, I used to hear the buzzing loom and the women's voices under my own roof. Shall I never hear them again, nor taste those nice little savory dishes which my dearest wife knew how to serve up?"

"Tush! we shall fare better here," said another. "But how innocently those women are babbling together, without guessing that we overhear them! And mark that richest voice of all, so pleasant and familiar, but which yet seems to have the authority of a mistress among them. Let us show ourselves at once. What harm can the lady of the palace and her maidens do to mariners and warriors like us?"

"Remember," said Eurylochus, "that it was a young maiden who beguiled three of our friends into the palace of the king of the Læstrygones, who ate up one of them in the twinkling of an eye."

No warning or persuasion, however, had any effect on his companions. They went up to a pair of folding doors at the farther end of the hall, and throwing them wide open, passed into the next room. Eurylochus meanwhile had stepped behind a pillar. In the short moment while the folding doors opened and closed again, he caught a glimpse of a very beautiful woman rising from the loom, and coming to meet the poor weather-beaten wanderers, with a hospitable smile and her hand stretched out in welcome. There were four other young women, who joined their hands and danced merrily forward, making gestures of obeisance to the strangers. They were only less beautiful than the lady who seemed to be their mistress. Yet Eurylochus fancied that one of them had sea-green hair and that the close-fitting bodice of a second looked like the bark of a tree and that both the others had something odd in their aspect, although he could not quite determine what it was, in the little while that he had to examine them.

The folding doors swung quickly back and left him standing behind the pillar, in the solitude of the outer hall. There Eurylochus waited until he was quite weary, and listened eagerly to every sound, but without hearing anything that could help him to guess what had become of his friends. Footsteps, it is true, seemed to be passing and repassing in other parts of the palace. Then there was a clatter of silver dishes, or golden ones, which made him imagine a rich feast in a splendid banqueting hall. But by and by he heard a tremendous grunting and squealing, and then a sudden scampering, like that of small, hard hoofs over a marble floor, while the voices of the mistress and her four handmaidens were screaming all together, in tones of anger and derision. Eurylochus could not conceive what had happened unless a drove of swine had broken into the palace, attracted by the smell of the feast. Chancing to cast his eyes at the fountain, he saw that it did not shift its shape, as formerly, nor looked either like a long-robed man or a lion, a tiger, a wolf, or an ass. It looked like nothing but a hog, which lay wallowing in the marble basin, and filled it from brim to brim.

But we must leave the prudent Eurylochus waiting in the outer hall and follow his friends into the inner secrecy of the palace. As soon as the beautiful woman saw them, she arose from the loom, as I have told you, and came forward, smiling, and stretching out her hand. She took the hand of the foremost among them, and bade him and the whole party welcome.

"You have been long expected, my good friends," said she. "I and my maidens are well acquainted with you, although you do not appear to recognize us. Look at this piece of tapestry, and judge if your faces must not have been familiar to us."

The voyagers examined the web of cloth which the beautiful woman had been weaving in her loom; and, to their vast astonishment, they saw their own figures perfectly represented in different colored threads. It was a lifelike picture of their recent adventures, showing them in the cave of Polyphemus, and how they had put out his one great moony eye; while in another part of the tapestry they were untying the leathern bags, puffed out with contrary winds; and farther on, they beheld themselves scampering away from the gigantic king of the Læstrygones, who had caught one of them by the leg. Lastly, there they were, sitting on the desolate shore of this very island, hungry and downcast, and looking ruefully at the bare bones of the stag which they devoured yesterday. This was as far as the work had yet proceeded; but when the beautiful woman should again sit down at her loom, she would probably make a picture of what had since happened to the strangers, and of what was now going to happen.

"You see," she said, "that I know all about your troubles; and you cannot doubt that I desire to make you happy for as long a time as you may remain with me. For this purpose, my honored guests, I have ordered a banquet to be prepared. Fish, fowl, and flesh, roasted and in luscious stews, and seasoned, I trust, to all your tastes, are ready to be served up. If your appetites tell you that it is dinner time, then come with me to the festal saloon."

At this kind invitation, the hungry mariners were quite overjoyed; and one of them, taking upon himself to be spokesman, assured their hospitable hostess that any hour of the day was dinner time with them, whenever they could get flesh to put in the pot, and fire to boil it with. The beautiful woman led the way; and the four maidens (one of them had sea-green hair, another a bodice of oak bark, a third sprinkled a shower of water drops from her fingers' ends, and the fourth had some other oddity, which I have forgotten), all these followed behind, and hurried the guests along, until they entered a magnificent saloon. It was built in a perfect oval and lighted from a crystal dome above. Around the walls were ranged two and twenty thrones, overhung by canopies of crimson and gold, and provided with the softest of cushions, which were tasseled and fringed with gold cord. Each of the strangers was invited to sit down; and there they were, two and twenty storm-beaten mariners, in worn and tattered garb, sitting on thrones so rich and gorgeous that the proudest monarch had nothing more splendid in his stateliest hall.

Then you might have seen the guests nodding, winking with one eye, and leaning from one

throne to another, to communicate their satisfaction in hoarse whispers.

"Our good hostess has made kings of us all,"
said one. "Ha! do you smell the feast? I'll
engage it will be fit to set before two and twenty
kings."

"I hope," said another, "it will be, mainly good
substantial joints, sirloins, spareribs, and hinder
quarters, without too many kickshaws. If I
thought the good lady would not take it amiss, I
should call for a fat slice of fried bacon to begin
with."

Ah, the gluttons and gormandizers! You see
how it was with them. In the loftiest seats of
dignity, on royal thrones, they could think of
nothing but their greedy appetite, which was the
portion of their nature that they shared with
wolves and swine; so that they resembled those
vilest of animals far more than they did kings —
if, indeed, kings were what they ought to be.

But the beautiful woman now clapped her
hands; and immediately there entered a train of
two and twenty serving men, bringing dishes of
the richest food, all hot from the kitchen fire,
and sending up such a steam that it hung like a
cloud below the crystal dome of the saloon. An
equal number of attendants brought great flagons
of wine, of various kinds, some of which sparkled
as it was poured out and went bubbling down the
throat; while of other sorts, the purple liquor was
so clear that you could see the wrought figures
at the bottom of the goblet. While the servants
supplied the two and twenty guests with food and
drink, the hostess and her four maidens went
from one throne to another, exhorting them to
eat their fill, and to quaff wine abundantly and

thus to recompense themselves, at this one banquet, for the many days when they had gone without a dinner. But, whenever the mariners were not looking at them (which was pretty often, as they looked chiefly into the basins and platters), the beautiful woman and her damsels turned aside and laughed. Even the servants, as they knelt down to present the dishes, might be seen to grin and sneer, while the guests were helping themselves to the offered dainties.

And, once in a while, the strangers seemed to taste something that they did not like.

"Here is an odd kind of spice in this dish," said one. "I can't say it quite suits my palate. Down it goes, however."

"Send a good draught of wine down your throat," said his comrade on the next throne. "That is the stuff to make this sort of cookery relish well. Though I must needs say, the wine has a queer taste, too. But the more I drink of it the better I like the flavor."

Whatever little fault they might find with the dishes, they sat at dinner a prodigiously long while; and it would really have made you ashamed to see how they swilled down the liquor and gobbled up the food. They sat on golden thrones, to be sure, but they behaved like pigs in a sty; and, if they had had their wits about them, they might have guessed that this was the opinion of their beautiful hostess and her maidens. It brings a blush into my face to reckon up in my own mind what mountains of meat and pudding and what gallons of wine these two and twenty guzzlers and gormandizers ate and drank. They forgot all about their homes and their wives and children, and all about Ulysses, and every-

thing else, except this banquet, at which they
wanted to keep feasting forever. But at length
they began to give over, from mere incapacity to
hold any more.

"That last bit of fat is too much for me!" said
one.

"And I have not room for another morsel." said
his next neighbor, heaving a sigh. "What a pity!
My appetite is as sharp as ever."

In short, they all left off eating and leaned
back on their thrones with such a stupid and
helpless aspect as made them ridiculous to
behold. When their hostess saw this, she laughed
aloud; so did her four damsels; so did the two and
twenty serving men that bore the dishes and
their two and twenty fellows that poured out the
wine. And the more loudly they all laughed, the
more stupid and helpless did the two and twenty
gormandizers look. Then the beautiful woman
took her stand in the middle of the saloon, and
stretching out a slender rod (it had been all the
while in her hand, although they never noticed it
till this moment), she turned it from one guest to
another, until each had felt it pointed at himself.
Beautiful as was her face, it looked just as
wicked and mischievous as the ugliest serpent
that ever was seen; and fat-witted as the
voyagers had made themselves, they began to
suspect that they had fallen into the power of an
evil-minded enchantress.

"Wretches," cried she, "you have abused a
lady's hospitality; and in this princely saloon your
behavior has been suited to a hogpen. You are
already swine in everything but the human form,
which you disgrace, and which I myself should be
ashamed to keep a moment longer, were you to

share it with me. But it will require only the slightest exercise of magic to make the exterior conform to the hoggish disposition. Assume your proper shapes, gormandizers, and begone to the sty!"

Uttering these last words, she waved her wand; and stamping her foot imperiously each of the guests was struck aghast at beholding, instead of his comrades in human shape, one and twenty hogs sitting on the same number of golden thrones. Each man (as he still supposed himself to be) essayed to give a cry of surprise, but found that he could merely grunt, and that, in a word, he was just such another beast as his companions. It looked so intolerably absurd to see hogs on cushioned thrones, that they made haste to wallow down upon all fours, like other swine. They tried to groan and beg for mercy, but forthwith emitted the most awful grunting and squealing that ever came out of swinish throats. They would have wrung their hands in despair, but, attempting to do so, grew all the more desperate for seeing themselves squatted on their hams and pawing the air with their fore trotters. Dear me! what pendulous ears they had! what little red eyes, half buried in fat! and what long snouts, instead of Grecian noses!

But brutes as they certainly were, they yet had enough of human nature in them to be shocked at their own hideousness; and, still intending to groan, they uttered a viler grunt and squeal than before. So harsh and ear-piercing it was, that you would have fancied a butcher was sticking his knife into each of their throats, or, at the very least, that somebody was pulling every hog by this funny little twist of a tail.

"Begone to your sty!" cried the enchantress, giving them some smart strokes with her wand; and then she turned to the serving men, "Drive out these swine, and throw down some acorns for them to eat."

The door of the saloon being flung open, the drove of hogs ran in all directions save the right one, in accordance with their hoggish perversity, but were finally driven into the back yard of the palace. It was a sight to bring tears into one's eyes (and I hope none of you will be cruel enough to laugh at it), to see the poor creatures go snuffing along, picking up here a cabbage leaf and there a turnip top and rooting their noses in the earth for whatever they could find. In their sty, moreover, they behaved more piggishly, snorted at one another, put their feet in the trough, and gobbled up their victuals in a ridiculous hurry; and, when there was nothing more to be had, they made a great pile of themselves among some unclean straw, and fell fast asleep. If they had any human reason left, it was just enough to keep them wondering when they should be slaughtered and what quality of bacon they should make.

Meantime, as I told you before, Eurylochus had waited and waited and waited in the entrance hall of the palace, without being able to comprehend what had befallen his friends. At last, when the swinish uproar resounded through the palace, and when he saw the image of a hog in the marble basin, he thought it best to hasten back to the vessel and inform the wise Ulysses of these marvelous occurrences. He ran as fast as he could down the steps and never stopped to draw breath till he reached the shore.

"Why do you come alone?" asked King Ulysses as soon as he saw him. "Where are your two and twenty comrades?"

At these questions, Eurylochus burst into tears.

"Alas! cried he, "I greatly fear that we shall never see one of their faces again."

Then he told Ulysses all that had happened, as far as he knew it, and added that he suspected the beautiful woman to be a vile enchantress, and the marble palace, magnificent as it looked, to be only a dismal cavern in reality. As for his companions, he could not imagine what had become of them, unless they had been given to the swine to be devoured alive. At this intelligence, all the voyagers were greatly affrighted. But Ulysses lost no time in girding on his sword and hanging his bow and quiver over his shoulders and taking a spear in his right hand. When his followers saw their wise leader making these preparations, they inquired whither he was going, and earnestly besought him not to leave them.

"You are our king," cried they; "and what is more, you are the wisest man in the whole world and nothing but your wisdom and courage can get us out of this danger. If you desert us and go to the enchanted palace, you will suffer the same fate as our poor companions, and not a soul of us will ever see our dear Ithaca again."

"As I am your king, answered Ulysses, "and wiser than any of you, it is, therefore, the more my duty to see what has befallen our comrades, and whether anything can yet be done to rescue them. Wait for me here until tomorrow. If I do not then return, you must hoist sail and endeavor to find your way to our native land. For my part,

I am answerable for the fate of these poor mariners, who have stood by my side in battle, and been so often drenched to the skin, along with me, by the same tempestuous surges. I will either bring them back with me or perish."

Had his followers dared, they would have detained him by force. But King Ulysses frowned sternly on them and shook his spear and bade them stop him at their peril. Seeing him so determined, they let him go, and sat down on the sand, as disconsolate a set of people as could be, waiting and praying for his return.

It happened to Ulysses, just as before, that, when he had gone a few steps from the edge of the cliff, the purple bird came fluttering toward him, crying, "Peep, peep, pe — weep!" and using all the art it could to persuade him to go no farther.

"What mean you, little bird?" cried Ulysses. "You are arrayed like a king in purple and gold and wear a golden crown upon your head. Is it because I too am a king that you desire so earnestly to speak with me? If you can talk in human language, say what you would have me do."

"Peep!" answered the purple bird, very dolorously. "Peep, peep, pe — we — ep!"

Certainly there lay some heavy anquish at the little bird's heart; and it was a sorrowful predicament that he could not, at least, have the consolation of telling what it was. But Ulysses had no time to waste in trying to get at the mystery. He therefore quickened his pace, and had gone a good way along the pleasant wood path, when there met him a young man of very brisk and intelligent aspect and clad in a rather singular garb. He wore a short cloak and a sort of cap that seemed to be furnished with a pair if wings; and from the lightness of his step, you would have supposed that there might likewise be wings on his feet. To enable him to walk still better (for he was always on one journey or another), he carried a winged staff, around which two serpents were wriggling and twisting. In short, I have said enough to make you guess that is was Quicksilver; and Ulysses (who knew him of old, and had learned a great deal of his wisdom from him) recognized him in a moment.

"Whither are you going in such a hurry, wise Ulysses?" asked Quicksilver. "Do you not know that this island is enchanted? The wicked enchantress (whose name is Circe, the sister of King AEetes) dwells in the marble palace which you see yonder among the trees. By her magic arts, she changes every human being into the brute beast or fowl whom he happens most to resemble."

"That little bird, which met me at the edge of the cliff," exclaimed Ulysses, "was he a human being once?"

"Yes," answered Quicksilver. "He was once a king, named Picus, and a pretty good sort of king too, only rather too proud of his purple robe and his crown and the golden chain about his neck; so he was forced to take the shape of a gaudy-feathered bird. The lions and wolves and tigers, who will come running to meet you, in front of the palace, were formerly fierce and cruel men, resembling in their dispositions the wild beasts whose forms they now rightfully wear."

"And my poor companions," said Ulysses. "Have they undergone a similar change, through the arts of this wicked Circe?"

"You well know what gormandizers they were," replied Quicksilver; and, rogue that he was, he could not help laughing at the joke. "So you will not be surprised to hear that they have all taken the shapes of swine! If Circe had never done anything worse, I really should not think her so very much to blame."

"But can I do nothing to help them?" inquired Ulysses.

"It will require all your wisdom," said Quicksilver, "and a little of my own into the bargain, to keep your royal and sagacious self from being transformed into a fox. But do as I bid you; and the matter may end better than it has begun."

While he was speaking, Quicksilver seemed to be in search of something; he went stooping along the ground, and soon laid his hand on a little plant with a snow-white flower, which he plucked and smelled. Ulysses had been looking at that very spot only just before; and it appeared to him that the plant had burst into full flower the instant Quicksilver touched it with his fingers.

"Take this flower, King Ulysses," said he. "Guard it as you do your eyesight; for I can assure you it is exceedingly rare and precious, and you might seek the whole earth over without ever finding another like it. Keep it in your hand and smell of it frequently after you enter the palace and while you are talking with the enchantress. Especially when she offers you food or a draught of wine out of her goblet, be careful to fill your nostrils with the flower's fragrance. Follow these directions and you may defy her magic arts to change you into a fox."

Quicksilver then gave him some further advice how to behave, and bidding him be bold and prudent, again assured him that, powerful as Circe was, he would have a fair prospect of coming safely out of her enchanted palace. After listening attentively, Ulysses thanked his good friend and resumed his way. But he had taken only a few steps when, recollecting some other questions which he wished to ask, he turned round again, and beheld nobody on the spot where Quicksilver had stood; for that winged cap of his and those winged shoes, with the help of the winged staff, had carried him quickly out of sight.

When Ulysses reached the lawn in front of the palace, the lions and other savage animals came bounding to meet him and would have fawned upon him and licked his feet. But the wise king struck at them with his long spear and sternly bade them begone out of his path; for he knew that they had once been bloodthirsty men and would now tear him limb from limb, instead of fawning upon him, could they do the mischief that was in their hearts. The wild beasts yelped and glared at him and stood at a distance while he ascended the palace steps.

On entering the hall, Ulysses saw the magic fountain in the center of it. The up-gushing water had now again taken the shape of a man in a long, white, fleecy robe, who appeared to be making gestures of welcome. The king likewise heard the noise of the shuttle in the loom and the sweet melody of the beautiful woman's song, and then the pleasant voices of herself and the four maidens talking together, with peals of merry laughter intermixed. But Ulysses did not waste much time in listening to the laughter or the song. He leaned his spear against one of the pillars of the hall, and then, after loosening his sword in the scabbard, stepped boldly forward and threw the folding doors wide open. The moment she beheld his stately figure standing in the doorway, the beautiful woman rose from the loom and ran to meet him with a glad smile throwing its sunshine over her face, and both her hands extended.

"Welcome, brave stranger!" cried she. "We were expecting you."

And the nymph with the sea-green hair made a curtsey down to the ground and likewise bade him welcome; so did her sister with the bodice of oaken bark and she that sprinkled dewdrops from her fingers' ends and the fourth one with some oddity which I cannot remember. And Circe, as the beautiful enchantress was called (who had deluded so many persons that she did not doubt of being able to delude Ulysses, not imagining how wise he was), again addressed him:

"Your companions," said she, "have already been received into my palace and have enjoyed the hospitable treatment to which the propriety of their behavior so well entitles them. If such be your pleasure, you shall first take some refreshment and then join them in the elegant apartments which they now occupy. See, I and my maidens have been weaving their figures into this piece of tapestry."

She pointed to the web of beautifully woven cloth in the loom. Circe and the four nymphs must have been very diligently at work since the arrival of the mariners; for a great many yards of tapestry had now been wrought, in addition to

what I before described. In this new part,
Ulysses saw his two and twenty friends represented as sitting on cushioned and canopied
thrones, greedily devouring dainties and quaffing
deep draughts of wine. The work had not yet
gone any further. Oh, no indeed. The enchantress was far too cunning to let Ulysses see the
mischief which her magic arts had since brought
upon the gormandizers.

"As for yourself, valiant sir," said Circe,
"judging by the dignity of your aspect, I take you
to be nothing less than a king. Deign to follow
me, and you shall be treated as befits your rank."

Ulysses followed her into the oval saloon,
where his two and twenty comrades had devoured
the banquet, which ended so disastrously for
themselves; but all this while, he had held the
snow-white flower in his hand, and had constantly smelled of it while Circe was speaking. As he
crossed the threshold of the saloon, he took good
care to inhale several long and deep snuffs of its
fragrance. Instead of two and twenty thrones,
which had before been ranged around the wall,
there was now only a single throne in the center
of the apartment. But this was surely the most
magnificent seat that ever a king or an emperor
reposed himself upon, all made of chased gold,
studded with precious stones, with a cushion that
looked like a soft heap of living roses, and
overhung by a canopy of sunlight which Circe
knew how to weave into drapery. The enchantress took Ulysses by the hand, and made
him sit down upon this dazzling throne. Then,
clapping her hands, she summoned the chief
butler.

"Bring hither," said she, "the goblet that is set

apart for kings to drink out of. And fill it with the same delicious wine which my royal brother, King AEtes, praised so highly, when he last visited me with my fair daughter Medea. That good and amiable child! Were she now here, it would delight her to see me offering this wine to my honored guest."

But Ulysses, while the butler was gone for the wine, held the snow-white flower to his nose.

"Is it a wholesome wine?" he asked.

At this the four maidens tittered; whereupon the enchantress looked round at them, with an aspect of severity.

"It is the wholesomest juice that ever was squeezed out of the grape," said she; "for, instead of disguising a man, as other liquor is apt to do, it brings him to his true self and shows him as he ought to be."

The chief butler liked nothing better than to see people turned into swine, or making any kind of beast of themselves; so he made haste to bring the royal goblet, filled with a liquid as bright as gold, and which kept sparkling upward and throwing a sunny spray over the brim. But, delightfully as the wine looked, it was mingled with the most potent enchantments that Circe knew how to concoct. For every drop of the pure grape juice there were two drops of the pure mischief; and the danger of the thing was that the mischief made it taste all the better. The mere smell of the bubbles, which effervesced at the brim, was enough to turn a man's beard into pig's bristles, or make a lion's claws grow out of his fingers, or a fox's brush behind him.

"Drink, my noble guest," said Circe, smiling as she presented him with the goblet. "You will find in this draught a solace for all your troubles."

King Ulysses took the goblet with his right hand, while with his left he held the snow-white flower to his nostrils, and drew in so long a breath that his lungs were quite filled with its pure and simple fragrance. Then, drinking off all the wine, he looked the enchantress calmly in the face.

"Wretch," cried Circe, giving him a smart stroke with her wand, "how dare you keep your human shape a moment longer? Take the form of the brute whom you most resemble. If a hog, go join your fellow swine in the sty; if a lion, a wolf, a tiger, go howl with the wild beasts on the lawn; if a fox, go exercise your craft in stealing poultry. Thou hast quaffed off my wine and canst be man no longer."

But such was the virtue of the snow-white flower that instead of wallowing down from his throne in swinish shape, or taking any other brutal form Ulysses looked even more manly and king-like than before. He gave the magic goblet a toss and sent it clashing over the marble floor, to the farthest end of the saloon. Then, drawing his sword, he seized the enchantress by her beautiful ringlets and made a gesture as if he meant to strike off her head at one blow.

"Wicked Circe," cried he, in a terrible voice, "this sword shall put an end to thy enchantments. Thou shalt die, vile wretch, and do no more mischief in the world, by tempting human beings into the vices which make beasts of them."

The tone and countenance of Ulysses were so awful and his sword gleamed so brightly and seemed to have so intolerably keen an edge, that

Circe was almost killed by the mere fright, without waiting for a blow. The chief butler scrambled out of the saloon, picking up the golden goblet as he went; and the enchantress and the four maidens fell on their knees, wringing their hands, and screaming for mercy.

"Spare me!" cried Circe. "Spare me, royal and wise Ulysses. For now I know that thou art he of whom Quicksilver forewarned me, the most prudent of mortals, against whom no enchantress can prevail. Thou only couldst have conquered Circe. Spare me, wisest of men. I will show thee true hospitality, and even give myself to be thy slave and this magnificent palace to be henceforth thy home."

The four nymphs, meanwhile, were making a most piteous ado; and especially the ocean nymph, with the sea-green hair, wept a great deal of salt water, and the fountain nymph, besides scattering dewdrops from her fingers' ends, nearly melted away into tears. But Ulysses would not be pacified until Circe had taken a solemn oath to change back his companions and as many others as he should direct, from their present forms of beast or bird into their former shapes of men.

"On these conditions," said he, "I consent to spare your life. Otherwise you must die upon the spot."

With a drawn sword hanging over her, the enchantress would readily have consented to do as much good as she had hitherto done mischief, however little she might like such employment. She therefore led Ulysses out of the back entrance of the palace and showed him the swine in their sty. There were about fifty of these unclean beasts in the whole herd; and though the greater part were hogs by birth and education, there was wonderfully little difference to be seen betwixt them and their new brethren who had so recently worn the human shape. To speak critically, indeed, the latter rather carried the thing to excess, and seemed to make it a point to wallow in the miriest part of the sty and otherwise to outdo the original swine in their own natural vocation. When men once turn to brutes, the trifle of man's wit that remains in them adds tenfold to their brutality.

The comrades of Ulysses, however, had not quite lost the remembrance of having formerly stood erect. When he approached the sty, two and twenty enormous swine separated themselves from the herd, and scampered toward him with such a chorus of horrible squealing as made him clap both hands to his ears. And yet they did not seem to know what they wanted, nor whether they were merely hungry or miserable from some other cause. It was curious, in the midst of their distress, to observe them thrusting their noses into the mire, in quest of something to eat. The nymph with the bodice of oaken bark (she was the hamadryad of an oak) threw a handful of acorns among them; and the two and twenty hogs scrambled and fought for the prize, as if they had tasted not so much as a noggin of sour milk for a twelvemonth.

"These must certainly be my comrades," said Ulysses. "I recognize their disposition. They are hardly worth the trouble of changing them into the human form again. Nevertheless, we will have it done, lest their bad example should corrupt the other hogs. Let them take their original shapes, therefore, Dame Circe, if your skill is equal to the task. It will require greater magic, I trow, than it did to make swine of them."

Circe waved her wand again and repeated a few magic words, at the sound of which the two and twenty hogs pricked up their pendulous ears. It was a wonder to behold how their snouts grew shorter and shorter, and their mouths (which they seemed to be sorry for, because they could not gobble so expeditiously) smaller and smaller, and how one and another began to stand upon his hind legs, and scratch his nose with his fore trotters. At first the spectators hardly knew whether to call them hogs or men, but by and by came to the conclusion that they rather resembled the latter. Finally, there stood the twenty-two comrades of Ulysses, looking pretty much the same as when they left the vessel.

You must not imagine, however, that the swinish quality had entirely gone out of them. When once it fastens itself into a person's character, it is very difficult getting rid of it. This was proved by the hamadryad, who, being exceedingly fond of mischief, threw another handful of acorns before the twenty-two newly restored people; whereupon down they wallowed, in a moment, and gobbled them up in a very shameful way. Then recollecting themselves, they scrambled to their feet and looked more than commonly foolish.

"Thanks, noble Ulysses!" they cried. "From brute beasts you have restored us to the condition of men again."

"Do not put yourselves to the trouble of thanking me," said the wise king. "I fear I have

"Spare me!" cried Circe.

"It was a wonder to behold their snouts
grow shorter and shorter."

done but little for you."

To say the truth, there was a suspicious kind of grunt in their voices, and for a long time afterwards they spoke gruffly and were apt to set up a squeal.

"It must depend upon your own future behavior," added Ulysses, "whether you do not find your way back to the sty."

At this moment, the note of a bird sounded from the branch of a neighboring tree.

"Peep, peep, pe — we — ep!"

It was the purple bird, who, all this while, had been sitting over their heads, watching what was going forward, and hoping that Ulysses would remember how he had done his utmost to keep him and his followers out of harm's way. Ulysses ordered Circe instantly to make a king of this good little fowl and leave him exactly as she found him. Hardly were the words spoken, and before the bird had time to utter another "Pe — weep," King Picus leaped down from the bough of the tree, as majestic a sovereign as any in the world, dressed in a long purple robe and gorgeous yellow stockings, with a splendidly wrought collar about his neck and a golden crown upon his head. He and King Ulysses exchanged with each other the courtesies which belong to their elevated rank. But from that time forth, King Picus was no longer proud of his crown and his trappings of royalty nor of the fact of his being a king; he felt himself merely the upper servant of his people, and that it must be his lifelong labor to make them better and happier.

As for the lions, tigers, and wolves (though Circe would have restored them to their former shapes at his slightest word), Ulysses thought it advisable that they should remain as they now were, and thus give warning of their cruel dispositions, instead of going about under the guise of men, and pretending to human sympathies, while their hearts had the blood-thirstiness of wild beasts. So he let them howl as much as they liked, but never troubled his head about them. And, when everything was settled according to his pleasure, he sent to summon the remainder of his comrades, whom he had left at the seashore. These being arrived, with the prudent Eurylochus at their head, they all made themselves comfortable in Circe's enchanted palace, until quite rested and refreshed from the toils and hardships of their voyage.

The Pomegranate Seeds

MOTHER CERES was exceedingly fond of her daughter Proserpina, and seldom let her go alone into the fields. But, just at the time when my story begins, the good lady was very busy, because she had the care of the wheat and the Indian corn and the rye and the barley and, in short, of the crops of every kind, all over the earth; and as the season has thus far been uncommonly backward, it was necessary to make the harvest ripen more speedily than usual. So she put on her turban, made of poppies (a kind of flower which she was always noted for wearing), and got into her car drawn by a pair of winged dragons and was just ready to set off.

"Dear mother," said Proserpina, "I shall be very lonely while you are away. May I not run down to the shore and ask some of the sea nymphs to come up out of the waves to play with me?"

"Yes, child," answered Mother Ceres. "The sea nymphs are good creatures and will never lead you into any harm, but you must take care not to stray away from them, nor go wandering about the fields by yourself. Young girls, without their mothers to take care of them, are very apt to get into mischief."

The child promised to be as prudent as if she were a grown-up woman; and by the time the winged dragons had whirled the car out of sight, she was already on the shore, calling to the sea nymphs to come to play with her. They knew Proserpina's voice, and were not long in showing their glistening faces and sea-green hair above the water, at the bottom of which was their home. They brought along with them a great many beautiful shells; and sitting down on the moist sand, where the surf wave broke over them, they busied themselves in making a necklace, which they hung round Proserpina's neck. By way of showing her gratitude, the child besought them to go with her a little way into the fields, so that they might gather abundance of flowers, with which she would make each of her kind playmates a wreath.

"Oh, no, dear Proserpina," cried the sea nymphs; "we dare not go with you upon the dry land. We are apt to grow faint, unless at every breath we can snuff up the salt breeze of the ocean. And don't you see how careful we are to let the surf wave break over us every moment or two, so as to keep ourselves comfortably moist? If it were not for that, we should soon look like bunches of uprooted seaweed dried in the sun."

"It is a great pity," said Proserpina. "But do you wait for me here, and I will run and gather my apron full of flowers and be back again before the surf wave has broken ten times over you. I long to make you some wreaths that shall be as lovely as this necklace of many-colored shells."

"We will wait, then," answered the sea nymphs. "But while you are gone, we may as well lie down on a bank of soft sponge, under the water. The air today is a little too dry for our comfort. But we will pop up our heads every few minutes to see if you are coming."

The young Proserpina ran quickly to a spot, where only the day before she had see a great many flowers. These, however, were now a little past their bloom; and wishing to give her friends the freshest and loveliest blossoms, she strayed farther into the fields, and found some that made her scream with delight. Never had she met with such exquisite flowers before — violets so large and fragrant — roses with so rich and delicate a blush —such superb hyacinths, and such aromatic pinks — and many others, some of which seemed to be of new shapes and colors. Two or three times, moreover, she could not help thinking that a tuft of most splendid flowers has suddenly sprouted out of the earth before her very eyes, as if on purpose to tempt her a few steps farther. Proserpina's apron was soon filled and brimming over with delightful blossoms. She was on the point of turning back in order to rejoin the sea nymphs and sit with them on the moist sands, all twining wreaths together. But, a little farther on, what should she behold? It was a large shrub, completely covered with the most magnificent flowers in the world.

"The darlings!" cried Proserpina; and then she thought to herself, "I was looking at that spot only a moment ago. How strange it is that I did not see the flowers!"

The nearer she approached the shrub, the more

attractive it looked, until she came quite close
to it; and then, although its beauty was richer
than words can tell, she hardly knew whether to
like it or not. It bore above a hundred flowers of
the most brilliant hues, and each different from
the others, but all having a kind of resemblance
among themselves, which showed them to be
sister blossoms. But there was a deep glossy
luster on the leaves of the shrub and on the
petals of the flowers, that made Proserpina
doubt whether they might not be poisonous. To
tell you the truth, foolish as it may seem, she
was half inclined to turn round and run away.

"What a silly child I am!" thought she, taking
courage. "It is really the most beautiful shrub
that ever sprang out of the earth. I will pull it
up by the roots, carry it home, and plant it in my
mother's garden."

Holding up her apron full of flowers with her
left hand, Proserpina seized the large shrub with
the other, and pulled and pulled, but was hardly
able to loosen the soil about its roots. What a
deep-rooted plant it was! Again the girl pulled
with all her might, and observed that the earth
began to stir and crack to some distance around
the stem. She gave another pull, but relaxed her
hold, fancying that there was a rumbling sound
right beneath her feet. Did the roots extend
down into some enchanted cavern? Then, laughing at herself for so childish a notion, she made
another effort; up came the shrub, and
Proserpina staggered back, holding the stem
triumphantly in her hand and gazing at the deep
hole which its roots had left in the soil.

Much to her astonishment, this hole kept
spreading wider and wider and growing deeper

and deeper, until it really seemed to have no
bottom; and all the while, there came a rumbling
noise out of its depths, louder and louder and
nearer and nearer and sounding like the tramp of
horses' hoofs and the rattling of wheels. Too
much frightened to run away, she stood straining
her eyes into this wonderful cavity, and soon saw
a team of four sable horses, snorting smoke out
of their nostrils and tearing their way out of the
earth, with a splendid golden chariot whirling at
their heels. They leaped out of the bottomless
hole, chariot and all; and there they were,
tossing their black manes, flourishing their black
tails, and curvetting with every one of their
hoofs off the ground at once, close by the spot
where Proserpina stood. In the chariot sat the
figure of a man, richly dressed, with a crown on
his head, all flaming with diamonds. He was of a
noble aspect and rather handsome, but looked
sullen and discontented; and he kept rubbing his
eyes and shading them with his hand, as if he did
not live enough in the sunshine to be very fond of
its light.

As soon as this personage saw the affrighted
Proserpina, he beckoned her to come a little
nearer.

"Do not be afraid," said he, with as cheerful a
smile as he knew how to put on. "Come! Will
not you like to ride a little way with me in my
beautiful chariot?"

But Proserpina was so alarmed that she wished
for nothing but to get out of his reach. And no
wonder. The stranger did not look remarkably
good-natured, in spite of his smile; and as for his
voice, its tones were deep and stern and sounded
as much like the rumbling of an earthquake

underground as anything else. As is always the case with children in trouble, Proserpina's first thought was to call for her mother.

"Mother, Mother Ceres!" cried she, all in a tremble. "Come quickly and save me."

But her voice was too faint for her mother to hear. Indeed, it is most probable that Ceres was then a thousand miles off, making the corn grow in some far-distant country. Nor could it have availed her poor daughter, even had she been within hearing; for no sooner did Proserpina begin to cry out than the stranger leaped to the ground, caught the child in his arms, and again mounting the chariot, shook the reins and shouted to the four black horses to set off. They immediately broke into so swift a gallop that it seemed rather like flying through the air than running along the earth. In a moment, Proserpina lost sight of the pleasant vale of Enna, in which she had always dwelt. Another instant, and even the summit of Mount AEtna had become so blue in the distance that she could scarcely distinguish it from the smoke that gushed out of its crater. But still the poor child screamed, and scattered her apron full of flowers along the way and left a long cry trailing behind the chariot: and many mothers, to whose ears it came, ran quickly to see if any mischief had befallen their children. But Mother Ceres was a great way off and could not hear the cry.

As they rode on, the stranger did his best to soothe her.

"Why should you be so frightened, my pretty child?" said he, trying to soften his rough voice. "I promise not to do you any harm. What! You have been gathering flowers? Wait till we come to my palace, and I will give you a garden full of prettier flowers than those, all made of pearls and diamonds and rubies. Can you guess who I am? They call my name Pluto, and I am the king of diamonds and all other precious stones. Every atom of the gold and silver that lies under the earth belongs to me, to say nothing of the copper and iron and of the coal mines, which supply me with abundance of fuel. Do you see this splendid crown upon my head? You may have it for a plaything. Oh, we shall be very good friends, and you will find me more agreeable than you expect, when once we get out of this troublesome sunshine."

"Let me go home!" cried Proserpina. "Let me go home!"

"My home is better than your mother's," answered King Pluto. "It is a palace, all made of gold, with crystal windows; and because there is little or no sunshine thereabouts, the apartments are illuminated with diamond lamps. You never saw anything half so magnificent as my throne. If you like, you may sit down on it and be my little queen, and I will sit on the footstool."

"I don't care for golden palaces and thrones," sobbed Proserpina. "Oh, my mother, my mother! Carry me back to my mother!"

But King Pluto, as he called himself, only shouted to his steeds to go faster.

"Pray do not be foolish, Proserpina," said he, in rather a sullen tone. "I can offer you my palace and my crown and all the riches that are under the earth; and you treat me as if I were doing you an injury. The one thing which my palace needs is a merry little maid, to run up stairs and down and cheer up the rooms with her smile.

And this is what you must do for King Pluto."

"Never!" answered Proserpina, looking as miserable as she could. "I shall never smile again till you set me down at my mother's door."

But she might just as well have talked to the wind that whistled past them; for Pluto urged on his horses and went faster than ever. Proserpina continued to cry out, and screamed so long and so loudly that her poor little voice was almost screamed away; and when it was nothing but a whisper, she happend to cast her eyes over a great, broad field of waving grain — and whom do you think she saw? Who, but Mother Ceres, making the corn grow, and too busy to notice the golden chariot as it went rattling along. The child mustered all her strength and gave one more scream, but she was out of sight before Ceres had time to turn her head.

King Pluto had taken a road which now began to grow excessively gloomy. It was bordered on each side with rocks and precipices, between which the rumbling of the chariot wheels was reverberated with a noise like rolling thunder. The trees and bushes that grew in the crevices of the rocks had very dismal foliage; and by and by, although it was hardly noon, the air became obscured with a gray twilight. The black horses had rushed along so swiftly that they were already beyond the limits of the sunshine. But the duskier it grew the more did Pluto's visage assume an air of satisfaction. After all, he was not an ill-looking person, especially when he left off twisting his features into a smile that did not belong to them. Proserpina peeped at his face through the gathering dusk and hoped that he might not be so very wicked as she at first thought him.

"Ah, this twilight is truly refreshing," said King Pluto, "after being so tormented with that ugly and impertinent glare of the sun. How much more agreeable is lamplight or torchlight, more particularly when reflected from diamonds! It will be a magnificent sight when we get to my palace."

"Is it much farther?" asked Proserpina. "And will you carry me back when I have seen it?"

"We will talk of that by and by," answered Pluto. "We are just entering my dominions. Do you see that tall gateway before us? When we pass those gates, we are at home. And there lies my faithful mastiff at the threshold. Cerberus! Cerberus! Come hither, my good dog!"

So saying, Pluto pulled at the reins and stopped the chariot right between the tall, massive pillars of the gateway. The mastiff of which he had spoken got up from the threshold and stood on his hinder legs, so as to put his fore paws on the chariot wheel. But, my stars, what a strange dog it was! Why, he was a big, rough, ugly-looking monster, with three separate heads, and each of them fiercer than the two others; but, fierce as they were, King Pluto patted them all. He seemed as fond of his three-headed dog as if it had been a sweet little spaniel, with silken ears and curly hair. Cerberus, on the other hand, was evidently rejoiced to see his master, and expressed his attachment, as other dogs do, by wagging his tail at a great rate. Proserpina's eyes being drawn to it by its brisk motion, she saw that this tail was neither more nor less than a live dragon, with fiery eyes, and fangs that had a very poisonous aspect. And while the three-

headed Cerberus was fawning so lovingly on King
Pluto, there was the dragon tail wagging against
its will, and looking as cross and ill-natured as
you can imagine, on its own separate account.

"Will the dog bite me?" asked Proserpina,
shrinking closer to Pluto. "What an ugly creature
he is!"

"Oh, never fear," answered her companion.
"He never harms people, unless they try to enter
my dominions without being sent for, or to get
away when I wish to keep them here. Down,
Cerberus! Now, my pretty Proserpina, we will
drive on."

On went the chariot, and King Pluto seemed
greatly pleased to find himself once more in his
own kingdom. He drew Proserpina's attention to
the rich veins of gold that were to be seen among
the rocks, and pointed to several places where
one stroke of a pickax would loosen a bushel of
diamonds. All along the road, indeed, there were
sparkling gems, which would have been of inestimable value, above ground, but which were here
reckoned of the meaner sort, and hardly worth a
beggar's stooping for.

Not far from the gateway, they came to a
bridge, which seemed to be built of iron. Pluto
stopped the chariot and bade Proserpina look at
the stream which was gliding so lazily beneath it.
Never in her life had she beheld so torpid, so
black, so muddy-looking a stream. Its waters
reflected no images of anything that was on the
banks, and it moved as sluggishly as if it had
quite forgotten which way it ought to flow, and
had rather stagnate than flow either one way or
the other.

"This is the river Lethe," observed King Pluto.

"Is it not a very pleasant stream?"

"I think it a very dismal one," said Proserpina.

"It suits my taste, however," answered Pluto,
who was apt to be sullen when anybody disagreed
with him. "At all events, its water has one very
excellent quality; a single draught of it makes
people forget every care and sorrow that has
hitherto tormented them. Only sip a little of it,
my dear Proserpina, and you will instantly cease
to grieve for your mother, and will have nothing
in your memory that can prevent your being
perfectly happy in my palace. I will send for
some, in a golden goblet, the moment we arrive."

"Oh, no, no, no!" cried Proserpina, weeping
afresh. "I had a thousand times rather be
miserable with remembering my mother, than be
happy in forgetting her. That dear, dear mother!
I never, never, will forget her."

"We shall see," said King Pluto. "You do not
know what fine times we will have in my palace.
Here we are just at the portal. These pillars are
solid gold, I assure you."

He alighted from the chariot, and taking
Proserpina in his arms, carried her up a lofty
flight of steps into the great hall of the palace.
It was splendidly illuminated by means of large
precious stones, of various hues, which seemed to
burn like so many lamps, and glowed with a
hundredfold radiance all through the vast apartment. And yet there was a kind of gloom in the
midst of this enchanted light; nor was there a
single object in the hall that was really agreeable
to behold, except the little Proserpina herself, a
lovely child, with one earthly flower which she
had not let fall from her hand. It is my opinion
that even King Pluto had never been happy in his

palace, and that this was the true reason why he had stolen away Proserpina, in order that he might have something to love, instead of cheating his heart any longer with this tiresome magnificence.   And, though he pretended to dislike the sunshine of the upper world, yet the effect of the child's presence, bedimmed as she was by her tears, was as if a faint and watery sunbeam had somehow or other found its way into the enchanted hall.

Pluto now summoned his domestics, and bade them lose no time in preparing a most sumptuous banquet, and above all things, not to fail of setting a golden beaker of the water of Lethe by Proserpina's plate.

"I will neither drink that nor anything else," said Proserpina.   "Nor will I taste a morsel of food, even if you keep me forever in your palace."

"I should be sorry for that." replied King Pluto, patting her cheek; for he really wished to be kind, if he had only known how.   "You are a spoiled child, I perceive, my little Proserpina; but when you see the nice things which my cook will make for you, your appetite will quickly come again."

Then, sending for the head cook, he gave strict orders that all sorts of delicacies, such as young people are usually fond of, should be set before Proserpina. He had a secret motive in this; for, you are to understand, it is a fixed law, that, when persons are carried off to the land of magic, if they once taste any food there, they can never get back to their friends. Now, if King Pluto had been cunning enough to offer Proserpina some fruit, or bread and milk (which was the simple fare to which the child had always been accustomed), it is very probable that she would soon have been tempted to eat it. But he left the matter entirely to his cook, who, like all other cooks, considered nothing fit to eat unless it were rich pastry, or highly seasoned meat, or spiced sweet cakes — things which Proserpina's mother had never given her, and the smell of which quite took away her appetite, instead of sharpening it.

But my story must now clamber out of King Pluto's dominions, and see what Mother Ceres has been about, since she was bereft of her daughter. We had a glimpse of her, as you remember, half hidden among the waving grain, while the four black steeds were swiftly whirling along the chariot, in which her beloved Proserpina was so unwillingly borne away. You recollect, too, the loud scream which Proserpina gave, just when the chariot was out of sight.

Of all the child's outcries, this last shriek was the only one that reached the ears of Mother Ceres. She had mistaken the rumbling of the chariot wheels for a peal of thunder, and imagined that a shower was coming up, and that it would assist her in making the corn grow. But, at the sound of Proserpina's shriek, she started, and looked about in every direction, not knowing whence it came, but feeling almost certain that it was her daughter's voice. It seemed so unaccountable, however, that the girl should have strayed over so many lands and seas (which she herself could not have traversed without the aid of her winged dragons) that the good Ceres tried to believe that it must be the child of some other parent, and not her own darling Proserpina, who had uttered this lamentable cry. Nevertheless, it troubled her with a vast many tender fears, such as are ready to bestir themselves in every mother's heart, when she finds it necessary to go away from her dear children without leaving them under the care of some maiden aunt, or other such faithful guardain. So she quickly left the field in which she had been so busy; and, as her work was not half done, the grain looked next day as if it needed both sun and rain, and as if it were blighted in the ear and had something the matter with its roots.

The pair of dragons must have had very nimble wings; for, in less than an hour, Mother Ceres had alighted at the door of her home and found it empty. Knowing, however, that the child was fond of sporting on the seashore, she hastened thither as fast as she could, and there beheld the wet faces of the poor sea nymphs peeping over a wave. All this while, the good creatures had been waiting on the bank of sponge, and, once every half minute or so, has popped up their four heads above water, to see if their playmate were yet coming back. When they saw Mother Ceres, they sat down on the crest of the surf wave and let it toss them ashore at her feet.

"Where is Proserpina?" cried Ceres. "Where is my child? Tell me, you naughty sea nymphs, have you enticed her under the sea?"

"Oh, no, good Mother Ceres," said the innocent sea nymphs, tossing back their green ringlets and looking her in the face. "We never should dream of such a thing. Proserpina has been at play with us, it is true; but she left us a long while ago, meaning only to run a little way upon the dry land and gather some flowers for a wreath. This was early in the day, and we have seen nothing of her since."

Ceres scarcely waited to hear what the nymphs had to say, before she hurried off to make inquiries all through the neighborhood. But nobody told her anything that could enable the poor mother to guess what had become of Proserpina. A fisherman, it is true, had noticed her little footprints in the sand, as he went homeward along the beach with a basket of fish; a rustic had seen the child stooping to gather flowers; several persons had heard either the rattling of chariot wheels or the rumbling of distant thunder; and one old woman, while plucking vervain and catnip, had heard a scream, but supposed it to be some childish nonsense, and therefore did not take the trouble to look up. The stupid people! It took them such a tedious while to tell the nothing that they knew, that it was dark night before Mother Ceres found out that she must seek her daughter elsewhere. So she lighted a torch and set forth, resolving never to come back until Proserpina was discovered.

In her haste and trouble of mind, she quite forgot her car and the winged dragons; or, it may be, she thought that she could follow up the search more thoroughly on foot. At all events, this was the way in which she began her sorrowful journey, holding her torch before her and looking carefully at every object along the path. And as it happened, she had not gone far before she found one of the magnificent flowers which grew on the shrub that Proserpina had pulled up.

"Ha!" thought Mother Ceres, examining it by torchlight. "Here is the mischief in this flower!

The earth did not produce it by any help of mine, nor of its own accord.   It is the work of enchantment, and is therefore poisonous; and perhaps it has poisoned my poor child."

But she put the poisonous flower in her bosom, not knowing whether she might ever find any other memorial of Proserpina.

All night long at the door of every cottage and farmhouse, Ceres knocked, and called up the weary laborers to inquire if they had seen her child; and they stood, gaping and half asleep, at the threshold, and answered her pityingly and besought her to come in and rest. At the portal of every palace, too, she made so loud a summons that the menials hurried to throw open the gate, thinking that it must be some great king or queen, who would demand a banquet for supper and a stately chamber to repose in. And when they saw only a sad and anxious woman, with a torch in her hand and a wreath of withered poppies on her head, they spoke rudely and sometimes threatened to set the dogs upon her. But nobody had seen Proserpina nor could give Mother Ceres the least hint which way to seek her. Thus passed the night; and still she continued her search without sitting down to rest or stopping to take food, or even remembering to put out the torch; although first the rosy dawn and then the glad light of the morning sun made its red flame look thin and pale. But I wonder what sort of stuff this torch was made of; for it burnt dimly through the day and at night was as bright as ever, and never was extinguished by the rain or wind, in all the weary days and nights while Ceres was seeking for Proserpina.

It was not merely of human beings that she

asked tidings of her daughter. In the woods and
by the streams, she met creatures of another
nature, who used, in those old times to haunt the
pleasant and solitary places, and were very
sociable with persons who understood their
language and customs, as Mother Ceres did.
Sometimes, for instance, she tapped with her
finger against the knotted trunk of a majestic
oak; and immediately its rude bark would cleave
asunder, and forth would step a beautiful maiden,
who was the hamadryad of the oak, dwelling
inside it, and sharing its long life and rejoicing
when its green leaves sported with the breeze.
But not one of these leafy damsels had seen
Proserpina. Then, going a little farther, Ceres
would, perhaps, come to a fountain, gushing out
of a pebbly hollow in the earth and would dabble
with her hand in the water. Behold, up through
its sandy and pebbly bed, along with the
fountain's gush, a young woman with dripping
hair would arise, and stand gazing at Mother
Ceres, half out of the water, and undulating up
and down with its ever-restless motion. But
when the mother asked whether the poor lost
child had stopped to drink out of the fountain,
the naiad, with weeping eyes (for these water
nymphs had tears to spare for everybody's grief),
would answer, "No!" in a murmuring voice, which
was just like the murmur of the stream.

Often, likewise, she encountered fauns, who
looked like sunburnt country people, except that
they had hairy ears and little horns upon their
foreheads, and the hinder legs of goats, on which
they gamboled merrily about the woods and
fields. They were a frolicsome kind of creature,
but grew as sad as their cheerful dispositions

would allow, when Ceres inquired for her
daughter, and they had no good news to tell. But
sometimes she came suddenly upon a rude gang
of satyrs who had faces like monkeys and horses'
tails behind them, and who were generally
dancing in a very boisterous manner, with shouts
of noisy laughter. When she stopped to question
them, they would only laugh the louder and make
new merriment out of the lone woman's distress.
How unkind of those ugly satyrs!   And once,
while crossing a solitary sheep pasture, she saw a
personage named Pan, seated at the foot of a tall
rock, and making music on a shepherd's flute.
He, too, had horns and hairy ears and goat's feet;
but, being acquainted with Mother Ceres, he
answered her question as civilly as he knew how,
and invited her to taste some milk and honey out
of a wooden bowl. But neither could Pan tell her
what had become of Proserpina, any better than
the rest of these wild people.

And thus Mother Ceres went wandering about
for nine long days and nights, finding no trace of
Proserpina, unless it were now and then a
withered flower; and these she picked up and put
in her bosom, because she fancied that they
might have fallen from her poor child's hand. All
day she traveled onward through the hot sun; and
at night, again, the flame of the torch would
redden and gleam along the pathway, and she
continued her search by its light, without ever
sitting down to rest.

On the tenth day, she chanced to espy the
mouth of a cavern, within which (though it was
bright noon everywhere else) there would have
been only a dusky twilight; but it so happened
that a torch was burning there. It flickered and

struggled with the duskiness, but could not half
light up the gloomy cavern with all its melancholy glimmer. Ceres was resolved to leave no
spot without a search; so she peeped into the
entrance of the cave and lighted it up a little
more, by holding her own torch before her. In so
doing, she caught a glimpse of what seemed to be
a woman, sitting on the brown leaves of the last
autumn, a great heap of which had been swept
into the cave by the wind. This woman (if
woman it were) was by no means so beautiful as
many of her sex; for her head, they tell me, was
shaped very much like a dog's, and, by way of
ornament, she wore a wreath of snakes around it.
But Mother Ceres, the moment she saw her knew
that this was an odd kind of person, who put all
her enjoyment in being miserable, and never
would have a word to say to other people, unless
they were as melancholy and wretched as she
herself delighted to be.

"I am wretched enough now," thought poor
Ceres, "to talk with this melancholy Hecate,
were she ten times sadder than ever she was
yet."

So she stepped into the cave, and sat down on
the withered leaves by the dog-headed woman's
side. In all the world, since her daughter's loss,
she had found no other companion.

"O Hecate," said she, "if ever you lose a
daughter, you will know what sorrow is. Tell me
for pity's sake, have you seen my poor child
Proserpina pass by the mouth of your cavern?"

"No," answered Hecate, in a cracked voice and
sighing betwixt every word or two; "no, Mother
Ceres, I have see nothing of your daughter. But
my ears, you must know, are made in such a way

that all cries of distress and affright, all over the
world, are pretty sure to find their way to them;
and nine days ago, as I sat in my cave, making
myself very miserable, I heard the voice of a
young girl, shrieking as if in great distress.
Something terrible has happened to the child, you
may rest assured. As well as I could judge, a
dragon, or some other cruel monster, was carrying her away."

"You kill me by saying so," cried Ceres, almost
ready to faint. "Where was the sound, and which
way did it seem to go?"

"It passed very swiftly along," said Hecate,
"and, at the same time, there was a heavy
rumbling of wheels toward the eastward. I can
tell you nothing more, except that, in my honest
opinion, you will never see your daughter again.
The best advice that I can give you is to take up
your abode in this cavern, where we will be the
two most wretched women in the world."

"Not yet, dark Hecate," replied Ceres. "But do
you first come with your torch and help me to
seek for my lost child. And when there shall be
no more hope of finding her (if that black day is
ordained to come), then, if you will give me room
to fling myself down, either on those withered
leaves or on the naked rock, I will show you what
it is to be miserable. But until I know that she
has perished from the face of the earth, I will
not allow myself space even to grieve."

The dismal Hecate did not much like the idea
of going abroad into the sunny world. But then
she reflected that the sorrow of the disconsolate
Ceres would be like a gloomy twilight round
about them both, let the sun shine ever so
brightly, and that therefore she might enjoy her

bad spirits quite as well as if she were to stay in the cave. So she finally consented to go, and they set out together, both carrying torches although it was broad daylight and clear sunshine. The torchlight seemed to make a gloom; so that the people whom they met along the road could not very distinctly see their figures; and, indeed, if they once caught a glimpse of Hecate, with the wreath of snakes round her forehead, they generally thought it prudent to run away, without waiting for a second glance.

As the pair traveled along in this woebegone manner, a thought struck Ceres.

"There is one person," she exclaimed, "who must have seen my poor child and can doubtless tell what has become of her. Why did not I think of him before? It is Phœbus."

"What," said Hecate, "the young man that always sits in the sunshine? Oh, pray do not think of going near him. He is gay, light, frivolous young fellow, and will only smile in your face. And besides, there is such a glare of the sun about him, that he will quite blind my poor eyes, which I have almost wept away already."

"You have promised to be my companion," answered Ceres. "Come, let us make haste, or the sunshine will be gone and Phœbus along with it."

Accordingly, they went along in quest of Phœbus, both of them sighing grievously, and Hecate, to say the truth, making a great deal worse lamentation than Ceres; for all the pleasure she had, you know, lay in being miserable, and therefore she made the most of it. By and by, after a pretty long journey, they arrived at the sunniest spot in the whole world. There they beheld a beautiful young man, with long, curling ringlets, which seemed to be made of golden sunbeams; his garments were like light summer clouds; and the expression of his face was so exceedingly vivid that Hecate held her hands before her eyes, muttering that he ought to wear a black veil. Phœbus (for this was the very person whom they were seeking) had a lyre in his hands, and was making its chords tremble with sweet music; at the same time singing a most exquisite song, which he had recently composed. For besides a great many other accomplishments, this young man was renowned for his admirable poetry.

As Ceres and her dismal companion approached him, Phœbus smiled on them so cheerfully that Hecate's wreath of snakes gave a spiteful hiss, and Hecate heartily wished herself back in her cave. But as for Ceres, she was too earnest in her grief either to know or care whether Phœbus smiled or frowned.

"Phœbus!" exclaimed she, "I am in great trouble and have come to you for assistance. Can you tell me what has become of my dear child Proserpina?"

"Proserpina! Proserpina, did you call her name?" answered Phœbus, endeavoring to recollect; for there was such a continual flow of pleasant ideas in his mind that he was apt to forget what had happened no longer ago than yesterday. "Ah, yes, I remember her now. A very lovely child, indeed. I am happy to tell you, my dear madam, that I did see the little Proserpina not many days ago. You may make yourself perfectly easy about her. She is safe, and in excellent hands."

"Oh, where is my dear child?" cried Ceres, clasping her hands and flinging herself at his feet.

"Why," said Phœbus — and as he spoke, he kept touching his lyre so as to make a thread of music run in and out among his words — "as the little damsel was gathering flowers (and she has really a very exquisite taste for flowers), she was suddenly snatched up by King Pluto and carried off to his dominions. I have never been in that part of the universe; but the royal palace, I am told, is built in a very noble style of architecture, and of the most splendid and costly materials. Gold, diamonds, pearls, and all manner of precious stones will be your daughter's ordinary playthings. I recommend to you, my dear lady, to give yourself no uneasiness. Proserpina's sense of beauty will be duly gratified, and even in spite of the lack of sunshine, she will lead a very enviable life."

"Hush! Say not such a word!" answered Ceres, indignantly. "What is there to gratify her heart? What are all the splendors you speak of, without affection? I must have her back again. Will you go with me, Phœbus, to demand my daughter of this wicked Pluto?"

"Pray, excuse me," replied Phœbus, with an elegant obeisance. "I certainly wish you success, and regret that my own affairs are so immediately pressing that I cannot have the pleasure of attending you. Besides, I am not upon the best of terms with King Pluto. His three-headed mastiff would never let me pass the gateway; for I should be compelled to take a sheaf of sunbeams with me, and those, you know, are forbidden things in Pluto's kingdom."

"Ah, Phœbus," said Ceres, with bitter meaning in her words, "you have a harp instead of a heart. Farewell."

"Will you not stay a moment," asked Phœbus, "and hear me turn the pretty and touching story of Proserpina into extemporary verses?"

But Ceres shook her head and hastened away, along with Hecate. Phœbus (who, as I have told you, was an exquisite poet) forthwith began to make an ode about the poor mothers grief; and, if we were to judge of his sensibility by this beautiful production, he must have been endowed with a very tender heart. But when a poet gets into the habit of using his heartstrings to make chords for his lyre, he may thrum upon them as much as he will, without any great pain to himself. Accordingly, though Phœbus sang a very sad song, he was as merry all the while as were the sunbeams amid which he dwelt.

Poor Mother Ceres had now found out what had become of her daughter, but she was not a whit happier than before. Her case, on the contrary, looked more desperate than ever. As long as Proserpina was above ground, there might have been hopes of regaining her. But now that the poor child was shut up within the iron gates of the king of the mines, at the threshold of which lay the three-headed Cerberus, there seemed no possibility of her ever making her escape. The dismal Hecate, who loved to take the darkest view of things, told Ceres that she had better come with her to the cavern and spend the rest of her life in being miserable. Ceres answered that Hecate was welcome to go back thither herself, but that, for her part, she would wander about the earth in quest of the entrance to King Pluto's dominions. And Hecate took her at her word, and hurried back to her beloved cave, frightening a great many little children with a glimpse of her dog's face, as she went.

Poor Mother Ceres! It is melancholy to think of her pursuing her toilsome way, all alone, and holding up that never-dying torch, the flame of which seemed an emblem of the grief and hope that burned together in her heart. So much did she suffer, that, though her aspect had been quite youthful when her troubles began, she grew to look like an elderly person in a very brief time. She cared not how she was dressed, nor had she ever thought of flinging away the wreath of withered poppies, which she put on the very morning of Proserpina's disappearance. She roamed about in so wild a way, and with her hair so disheveled, that people took her for some distracted creature, and never dreamed that this was Mother Ceres, who had the oversight of every seed which the husbandman planted. Nowadays, however, she gave herself no trouble about seedtime nor harvest, but left the farmers to take care of their own affairs, and the crops to fade or flourish, as the case might be. There was nothing, now, in which Ceres seemed to feel an interest, unless when she saw children at play, or gathering flowers along the wayside. Then, indeed she would stand and gaze at them with tears in her eyes. The children, too appeared to have a sympathy with her grief, and would cluster themselves in a little group about her knees, and look up wistfully in her face; and Ceres, after giving them a kiss all round, would

lead them to their homes and advise their
mothers never to let them stray out of sight.

"For if they do," said she, "it may happen to
you, as it has to me, that the iron-hearted King
Pluto will take a liking to your darlings, and
snatch them up in his chariot, and carry them
away."

One day, during her pilgrimage in quest of the
entrance to Pluto's kingdom, she came to the
palace of King Celeus, who reigned at Eleusis.
Ascending a lofty flight of steps she entered the
portal, and found the royal household in a very
great alarm about the queeen's baby. The infant,
it seems, was sickly (being troubled with its
teeth, I suppose), and would take no food, and
was all the time moaning with pain. The queen
— her name was Metanira — was desirous of
finding a nurse; and when she beheld a woman of
matronly aspect coming up the palace steps, she
thought, in her own mind, that here was the very
person whom she needed. So Queen Metanira ran
to the door, with the poor wailing baby in her
arms and besought Ceres to take charge of it, or,
at least, to tell her what would do it good.

"Will you trust the child entirely to me?" asked
Ceres.

"Yes, and gladly too," answered the queen, "if
you will devote all your time to him. For I can
see that you have been a mother."

"You are right," said Ceres.   "I once had a
child of my own. Well; I will be the nurse of this
poor, sickly boy. But beware, I warn you, that
you do not interfere with any kind of treatment
which I may judge proper for him. If you do so,
the poor infant must suffer for his mother's
folly."

Then she kissed the child and it seemed to do
him good; for he smiled and nestled closely into
her bosom.

So Mother Ceres set her torch in a corner
(where it kept burning all the while), and took up
her abode in the palace of King Celeus, as nurse
to the little Prince Demophoön. She treated him
as if he were her own child, and allowed neither
the king nor the queen to say whether he should
be bathed in warm or cold water, or what he
should eat or how often he should take the air or
when he should be put to bed. You would hardly
believe me, if I were to tell how quickly the baby
prince got rid of his ailments, and grew fat and
rosy and strong and how he had two rows of ivory
teeth in less time than any other little fellow,
before or since. Instead of the palest and
wretchedest and puniest imp in the world (as his
own mother confessed him to be when Ceres first
took him in charge), he was now a strapping
baby, crowing, laughing, kicking up his heels and
rolling from one end of the room to the other.
All the good women in the neighborhood crowded
to the palace, and held up their hands, in
unutterable amazement, at the beauty and
wholesomeness of this darling little prince.
Their wonder was the greater, because he was
never seen to taste any food; not even so much
as a cup of milk.

"Pray, nurse," the queen kept saying, "how is it
that you make the child thrive so?"

"I was a mother once," Ceres always replied;
"and having nursed my own child, I know what
other children need."

But Queen Metanira, as was very natural, had
a great curiosity to know precisely what the

nurse did to her child. One night, therefore, she hid herself in the chamber where Ceres and the little prince were accustomed to sleep. There was a fire in the chimney and it had now crumbled into great coals and embers, which lay glowing on the hearth, with a blaze flickering up now and then, and flinging a warm and ruddy light upon the walls. Ceres sat before the hearth with the child in her lap and the firelight making her shadow dance upon the ceiling overhead. She undressed the little prince and bathed him all over with some fragrant liquid out of a vase. The next thing she did was to rake back the red embers and make a hollow place among them, just where the backlog had been. At last, while the baby was crowing and clapping its fat little hands and laughing in the nurse's face (just as you may have seen your little brother or sister do before going into its warm bath), Ceres suddenly laid him, all naked as he was, in the hollow among the red-hot embers. She then raked the ashes over him and turned quietly away.

You may imagine, if you can, how Queen Metanira shrieked, thinking nothing less than that her dear child would be burned to a cinder. She burst forth from her hiding place and, running to the hearth, raked open the fire and snatched up poor little Prince Demophoön out of his bed of live coals, one of which he was gripping in each of his fists. He immediately set up a grievous cry, as babies are apt to do when rudely startled out of a sound sleep. To the queen's astonishment and joy, she could perceive no token of the child's being injured by the hot fire in which he had lain. She now turned to Mother Ceres and asked her to explain the mystery.

"Foolish woman," answered Ceres, "did you not promise to intrust this poor infant entirely to me? You little know the mischief you have done him. Had you left him to my care, he would have grown up like a child of celestial birth, endowed with superhuman strength and intelligence, and would have lived forever. Do you imagine that earthly children are to become immortal without being tempered to it in the fiercest heat of the fire? But you have ruined your own son. For though he will be a strong man and a hero in his day, yet, on account of your folly, he will grow old and finally die, like the sons of other women. The weak tenderness of his mother has cost the poor boy an immortality. Farewell."

Saying these words, she kissed the little Prince Demophoön, and sighed to think what he had lost, and took her departure without heeding Queen Metanira, who entreated her to remain and cover up the child among the hot embers as often as she pleased. Poor baby! He never slept so warmly again.

While she dwelt in the king's palace, Mother Ceres had been so continually occupied with taking care of the young prince that her heart was a little lightened of its grief for Proserpina. But now, having nothing else to busy herself about, she became just as wretched as before. At length, in her despair, she came to the dreadful resolution that not a stalk of grain nor a blade of grass, not a potato nor a turnip nor any other vegetable that was good for man or beast to eat, should be suffered to grow until her daughter were restored. She even forbade the flowers to bloom, lest somebody's heart should be cheered by their beauty.

Now, since not so much as a head of asparagus ever presumed to poke itself out of the ground, without the especial permission of Ceres, you may conceive what a terrible calamity had here fallen upon the earth. The husbandmen plowed and planted as usual; but there lay the rich black furrows, all as barren as a desert of sand. The pastures looked as brown in the sweet month of June as ever they did in chill November. The rich man's broad acres and the cottager's small garden patch were equally blighted. Every little girl's flower bed showed nothing but dry stalks. The old people shook their white heads and said that the earth had grown aged like themselves, and was no longer capable of wearing the warm smile of summer on its face. It was really piteous to see the poor, starving cattle and sheep, how they followed behind Ceres, lowing and bleating, as if their instinct taught them to expect help from her; and everybody that was acquainted with her power besought her to have mercy on the human race, and, at all events, to let the grass grow. But Mother Ceres, though naturally of an affectionate disposition, was now inexorable.

"Never," said she. "If the earth is ever again to see any verdure, it must first grow along the path which my daughter will tread in coming back to me."

Finally, as there seemed to be no other remedy, our old friend Quicksilver was sent posthaste to King Pluto, in hopes that he might be persuaded to undo the mischief he had done and to set everything right again, by giving up Proserpina. Quicksilver accordingly made the

best of his way to the great gate, took a flying
leap right over the three-headed mastiff, and
stood at the door of the palace in an inconceiv-
ably short time. The servants knew him both by
his face and garb; for his short cloak and his
winged cap and shoes and his snaky staff had
often been seen thereabouts in times gone by.
He requested to be shown immediately into the
king's presence; and Pluto, who heard his voice
from the top of the stairs, and who loved to
recreate himself with Quicksilver's merry talk,
called out to him to come up. And while they
settle their business together, we must inquire
what Proserpina has been doing ever since we
saw her last.

The child had declared, as you may remember,
that she would not taste a mouthful of food as
long as she should be compelled to remain in
King Pluto's palace. How she contrived to
maintain her resolution, and at the same time to
keep herself tolerably plump and rosy, is more
than I can explain; but some young ladies, I am
given to understand, possess the faculty of living
on air, and Proserpina seems to have possessed it
too. At any rate, it was now six months since
she left the outside of the earth; and not a
morsel, so far as the attendants were able to
testify, had yet passed between her teeth. This
was the more creditable to Proserpina, inasmuch
as King Pluto had caused her to be tempted, day
after day, with all manner of sweetmeats and
richly preserved fruits and delicacies of every
sort, such as young people are generally most
fond of. But her good mother had often told her
of the hurtfulness of these things; and for that
reason alone, if there had been no other, she

would have resolutely refused to taste them.

All this time, being of a cheerful and active disposition, the little damsel was not quite so unhappy as you may have supposed. The immense palace had a thousand rooms and was full of beautiful and wonderful objects. There was a never-ceasing gloom, it is true, which half hid itself among the innumerable pillars, gliding before the child as she wandered among them, and treading stealthily behind her in the echo of her footsteps. Neither was all the dazzle of the precious stones, which flamed with their own light, worth one gleam of natural sunshine; nor could the most brilliant of the many-colored gems, which Proserpina had for playthings, vie with the simple beauty of the flowers she used to gather. But still, wherever the girl went, among those gilded halls and chambers, it seemed as if she carried Nature and sunshine along with her, and as if she scattered dewy blossoms on her right hand and on her left. After Proserpina came, the palace was no longer the same abode of stately artifice and dismal magnificence that it had been. The inhabitants all felt this and King Pluto more than any of them.

"My own little Proserpina," he used to say, "I wish you could like me a little better. We gloomy and cloudy-natured persons have often as warm hearts at bottom as those of a more cheerful character. If you would only stay with me of your own accord, it would make me happier than the possession of a hundred such palaces as this."

"Ah," said Proserpina, "you should have tried to make me like you before carrying me off. And the best thing you can now do is to let me go

again. Then I might remember you sometimes
and think that you were as kind as you knew how
to be. Perhaps, too, one day or other, I might
come back and pay you a visit."

"No, no," answered Pluto, with his gloomy
smile, "I will not trust you for that. You are too
fond of living in the broad daylight and gathering
flowers. What an idle and childish taste that is!
Are not these gems, which I have ordered to be
dug for you, and which are richer than any in my
crown — are thy not prettier than a violet?"

"Not half so pretty," said Proserpina, snatching
the gems from Pluto's hand and flinging them to
the other end of the hall. "O my sweet violets,
shall I never see you again?"

And then she burst into tears. But young
people's tears have very little saltiness or acidity
in them, and do not inflame the eyes so much as
those of grown persons; so that it is not to be
wondered at, if, a few moments afterwards,
Proserpina was sporting through the hall almost
as merrily as she and the four sea nymphs had
sported along the edge of the surf wave. King
Pluto gazed after her and wished that he, too,
was a child. And little Proserpina, when she
turned about and beheld this great king standing
in his spendid hall, and looking so grand and so
melancholy and so lonesome, was smitten with a
kind of pity. She ran back to him, and, for the
first time in her life, put her small soft hand in
his.

"I love you a little," whispered she, looking up
in his face.

"Do you, indeed, my dear child?" cried Pluto,
bending his dark face down to kiss her; but
Proserpina shrank away from the kiss, for though

his features were noble, they were very dusky and grim. "Well, I have not deserved it of you, after keeping you a prisoner for so many months, and starving you, besides. Are you not terribly hungry? Is there nothing which I can get you to eat?"

In asking this question, the king of the mines had a very cunning purpose; for, you will recollect, if Proserpina tasted a morsel of food in his dominions, she would never afterwards be at liberty to quit them.

"No, indeed," said Proserpina. "Your head cook is always baking and stewing and roasting and rolling out paste and contriving one dish or another, which he imagines may be to my liking. But he might just as well save himself the trouble, poor, fat little man that he is. I have no appetite for anything in the world, unless it were a slice of bread of my mother's own baking, or a little fruit out of her garden."

When Pluto heard this, he began to see that he had mistaken the best method of tempting Proserpina to eat. The cook's made dishes and artificial dainties were not half so delicious, in the good child's opinion, as the simple fare to which Mother Ceres had accustomed her. Wondering that he had never thought of it before, the king now sent one of his trusty attendants, with a large basket, to get some of the finest and juiciest pears, peaches, and plums which could anywhere be found in the upper world. Unfortunately, however, this was during the time when Ceres had forbidden any fruits or vegetables to grow; and, after seeking all over the earth, King Pluto's servant found only a single pomegranate, and that so dried up as to be not worth eating. Nevertheless, since there was no better to be had, he brought this dry, old, withered pomegranate home to the palace, put it on a magnificent golden salver, and carried it up to Proserpina. Now it happened, curiously enough, that just as the servant was bringing the pomegranate into the back door of the palace, our friend Quicksilver had gone up the front steps, on his errand to get Proserpina away from King Pluto.

As soon as Proserpina saw the pomegranate on the golden salver, she told the servant that he had better take it away again.

"I shall not touch it, I assure you," said she. "If I were ever so hungry, I should never think of eating such a miserable, dry pomegranate as that."

"It is the only one in the world," said the servant.

He set down the golden salver, with the wizened pomegranate upon it, and left the room. When he was gone, Proserpina could not help coming close to the table and looking at this poor specimen of dried fruit with a great deal of eagerness; for, to say the truth, on seeing something that suited her taste, she felt all the six months' appetite taking possession of her at once. To be sure, it was a very wretched-looking pomegranate and seemed to have no more juice in it than an oyster shell. But there was no choice of such things in King Pluto's palace. This was the first fruit she had seen there, and the last she was ever likely to see; and unless she ate it immediately, it would grow drier than it already was, and be wholly unfit to eat.

"At least, I may smell it," thought Proserpina.

She took up the pomegranate and applied it to her nose. Somehow or other, being in such close neighborhood to her mouth, the fruit found its way into that little red cave. Dear me! what an everlasting pity! Before Proserpina knew what she was about, her teeth had actually bitten it, of their own accord. Just as this fatal deed was done, the door of the apartment opened, and in came King Pluto, followed by Quicksilver, who had been urging him to let his little prisoner go. At the first noise of their entrance, Proserpina withdrew the pomegranate from her mouth. But Quicksilver (whose eyes were very keen, and his wits the sharpest that ever anybody had) perceived that the child was a little confused; and seeing the empty salver, he suspected that she had been taking a sly nibble of something or other. As for honest Pluto, he never guessed at the secret.

"My little Proserpina," said the king, sitting down, and affectionately drawing her between his knees, "here is Quicksilver, who tells me that a great many misfortunes have befallen innocent people on account of my detaining you in my dominions. To confess the truth, I myself had already reflected that it was an unjustifiable act to take you away from your good mother. But, then, you must consider, my dear child, that this vast palace is apt to be gloomy (although the precious stones certainly shine very bright), and that I am not of the most cheerful disposition, and that, therefore, it was a natural thing enough to seek for the society of some merrier creature than myself. I hoped you would take my crown for a plaything and me — ah, you laugh, naughty Proserpina — me, grim as I am, for a playmate.

It was a silly expectation."

"Not so extremely silly," whispered Proserpina. "You have really amused me very much, some-times."

"Thank you," said King Pluto, rather dryly. "But I can see, plainly enough, that you think my palace a dusky prison, and me the iron-hearted keeper of it. And an iron heart I should surely have, if I could detain you here any longer, my poor child, when it is now six months since you tasted food. I give you your liberty. Go with Quicksilver. Hasten home to your dear mother."

Now although you may not have supposed it, Proserpina found it impossible to take leave of poor King Pluto without some regrets and a good deal of compunction for not telling him about the pomegranate. She even shed a tear or two, thinking how lonely and cheerless the great palace would seem to him, with all its ugly glare of artificial light, after she herself — his one little ray of natural sunshine, whom he had stolen, to be sure, but only because he valued her so much — after she should have departed. I know not how many kind things she might have said to the disconsolate king of the mines, had not Quicksilver hurried her away.

"Come along quickly," whispered he in her ear, "or his Majesty may change his royal mind. And take care, above all things, that you say nothing of what was brought you on the golden salver."

In a very short time, they had passed the great gateway (leaving the three-headed Cerberus barking and yelping and growling with threefold din, behind them), and emerged upon the surface of the earth. It was delightful to behold, as Proserpina hastened along, how the path grew verdant behind and on either side of her. Wherever she set her blessed foot, there was at once a dewy flower. The violets gushed up along the wayside. The grass and the grain began to sprout with tenfold vigor and luxuriance, to make up for the dreary months that had been wasted in barrenness. The starved cattle immediately set to work grazing, after their long fast, and ate enormously all day, and got up at midnight to eat more. But I can assure you it was a busy time of year with the farmers, when they found the summer coming upon them with such a rush. Nor must I forget to say that all the birds in the whole world hopped about upon the newly blossoming trees and sang together in a prodigious ecstasy of joy.

Mother Ceres had returned to her deserted home, and was sitting disconsolately on the doorstep, with her torch burning in her hand. She had been idly watching the flame for some moments past, when, all at once, it flickered and went out.

"What does this mean?" thought she. "It was an enchanted torch and should have kept burning till my child came back."

Lifting her eyes, she was surprised to see a sudden verdure flashing over the brown and barren fields, exactly as you may have observed a golden hue gleaming far and wide across the landscape from the just risen sun.

"Does the earth disobey me?" exclaimed Mother Ceres, indignantly. "Does it presume to be green, when I have bidden it be barren until my daughter shall be restored to my arms?"

"Then open your arms, dear mother," cried a well-known voice, "and take your little daughter into them."

And Proserpina came running and flung herself upon her mother's bosom. Their mutual transport is not to be described. The grief of their separation had caused both of them to shed a great many tears; now they shed a great many more, because their joy could not so well express itself in any other way.

When their hearts had grown a little more quiet, Mother Ceres looked anxiously at Proserpina.

"My child," said she, "did you taste any food while you were in King Pluto's palace?"

"Dearest mother," answered Proserpina, "I will tell you the whole truth. Until this very morning, not a morsel of food had passed my lips. But today they brought me a pomegranate (a very dry one it was, and all shriveled up, till there was little left of it but seeds and skin), and having seen no fruit for so long a time and being faint with hunger, I was tempted just to bite it. The instant I tasted it, King Pluto and Quicksilver came into the room. I had not swallowed a morsel; but — dear mother, I hope it was no harm — but six of the pomegranate seeds, I am afraid, remained in my mouth."

"Ah, unfortunate child, and miserable me!" exclaimed Ceres. "For each of those six pomegranate seeds you must spend one month of every year in King Pluto's palace. You are but half restored to your mother. Only six months with me and six with that good-for-nothing King of Darkness!"

"Do not speak so harshly of poor King Pluto," said Proserpina, kissing her mother. "He has some very good qualities; and I really think I can

bear to spend six months in his palace, if he will
only let me spend the other six with you.   He
certainly did very wrong to carry me off; but
then, as he says, it was but a dismal sort of life
for him, to live in that great gloomy place, all
alone; and it has made a wonderful change in his
spirits to have a little girl to run up stairs and
down.   There is some comfort in making him so
happy; and so, upon the whole, dearest mother,
let us be thankful that he is not to keep me the
whole year round."

The Golden Fleece

WHEN Jason, the son of the dethroned King of Iolchos, was a little boy, he was sent away from his parents and placed under the queerest school-master that ever you heard of. This learned person was one of the people, or quadrupeds, called Centaurs. He lived in a cavern, and had the body and legs of a white horse, with the head and shoulders of a man. His name was Chiron; and, in spite of his odd appearance, he was a very excellent teacher and had several scholars, who afterwards did him credit by making a great figure in the world. The famous Hercules was one, and so were Achilles and Philoctetes, likewise, and AEsculapius, who acquired immense repute as a doctor. The good Chiron taught his pupils how to play upon the harp and how to cure diseases and how to use the sword and shield, together with various other branches of education, in which the lads of those days used to be instructed, instead of writing and arithmetic.

I have sometimes suspected that Master Chiron was not really very different from other people, but that, being a kind-hearted and merry old fellow, he was in the habit of making believe that he was a horse, and scrambling about the schoolroom on all fours and letting the little boys ride upon his back. And so, when his scholars had grown up, and grown old and were trotting their grandchildren on their knees, they told them about the sports of their school days; and these young folks took the idea that their grandfathers had been taught their letters by a Centaur, half man and half horse. Little children, not quite understanding what is said to them, often get such absurd notions into their heads, you know.

Be that as it may, it has always been told for a fact (and always will be told, as long as the world lasts) that Chiron, with the head of a schoolmaster, had the body and legs of a horse. Just imagine the grave old gentleman clattering and stamping into the schoolroom on his four hoofs, perhaps treading on some little fellow's toes, flourishing his switch tail instead of a rod, and, now and then, trotting out of doors to eat a mouthful of grass! I wonder what the blacksmith charged him for a set of iron shoes!

So Jason dwelt in the cave with this four-footed Chiron, from the time that he was an infant, only a few months old, until he had grown to the full height of a man. He became a very good harper, I suppose, and skilful in the use of weapons and tolerably acquainted with herbs and other doctor's stuff, and, above all, an admirable horseman; for, in teaching young people to ride, the good Chiron must have been without a rival among schoolmasters. At length, being now a tall and athletic youth, Jason resolved to seek his fortune in the world, without asking Chiron's

advice, or telling him anything about the matter.
This was very unwise, to be sure; and I hope none
of you, my little hearers, will ever follow Jason's
example. But, you are to understand, he had
heard that he himself was a prince royal, and
that his father, King AEson, had been deprived of
the kingdom of Iolchos by a certain Pelias, who
would also have killed Jason, had he not been
hidden in the Centaur's cave. And, being come
to the strength of a man, Jason determined to
set all this business to rights, and to punish the
wicked Pelias for wronging his dear father, cast
him down from the throne, and seat himself
there instead.

With this intention, he took a spear in each
hand and threw a leopard's skin over his
shoulders, to keep off the rain, and set forth on
his travels, wiht his long yellow ringlets waving
in the wind. The part of his dress on which he
most prided himself was a pair of sandals that
had been his father's. They were handsomely
embroidered and were tied upon his feet with
strings of gold. But his whole attire was such as
people did not very often see; and as he passed
along, the women and children ran to the doors
and windows, wondering whither this beautiful
youth was journeying, with his leopard's skin and
his golden-tied sandals, and what heroic deeds he
meant to perform, with a spear in his right hand
and another in his left.

I know not how far Jason had traveled, when
he came to a turbulent river, which rushed right
across his pathway, with specks of white foam
among its black eddies, hurrying tumultuously
onward and roaring angrily as it went. Though
not a very broad river in the dry seasons of the

year, it was now swollen by heavy rains and by the melting of the snow on the sides of Mount Olympus. It thundered so loudly and looked so wild and dangerous, that Jason, bold as he was, thought it prudent to pause upon the brink. The bed of the stream seemed to be strewn with sharp and rugged rocks, some of which thrust themselves above the water. By and by, an uprooted tree, with shattered branches, came drifting along the current and got entangled among the rocks. Now and then, a drowned sheep, and once the carcass of a cow, floated past.

In short, the swollen river had already done a great deal of mischief. It was evidently too deep for Jason to wade and too boisterous for him to swim; he could see no bridge; and as for a boat, had there been any, the rocks would have broken it to pieces in an instant.

"See the poor lad," said a cracked voice close to his side. "He must have had but a poor education, since he does not know how to cross a little stream like this. Or is he afraid of wetting his fine golden-stringed sandals? It is a pity that his four-footed schoolmaster is not here to carry him safely across on his back!"

Jason looked round greatly surprised, for he did not know that anybody was near. But beside him stood an old woman, with a ragged mantle over her head, leaning on a staff, the top of which was carved into the shape of a cuckoo. She looked very aged and wrinkled and infirm; and yet her eyes, which were as brown as those of an ox, were so extremely large and beautiful that, when they were fixed on Jason's eyes, he could see nothing else but them. The old woman had a pomegranate in her hand, although the fruit was then quite out of season.

"Whither are you going, Jason?" she now asked.

She seemed to know his name, you will observe; and, indeed, those great brown eyes looked as if they had a knowledge of everything, whether past or to come. While Jason was gazing at her, a peacock strutted forward and took his stand at the old woman's side.

"I am going to Iolchos," answered the young man, "to bid the wicked King Pelias come down from my father's throne and let me reign in his stead."

"Ah, well, then," said the old woman, still with the same cracked voice, "if that is all your business, you need not be in a very great hurry. Just take me on your back, there's a good youth, and carry me across the river. I and my peacock have something to do on the other side, as well as yourself."

"Good mother," replied Jason, "your business can hardly be so important as the pulling down a king from his throne, Besides, as you may see for yourself, the river is very boisterous; and if I should chance to stumble, it would sweep both of us away more easily than it has carried off yonder uprooted tree. I would gladly help you if I could; but I doubt whether I am strong enough to carry you across."

"Then," said she, very scornfully, "neither are you strong enough to pull King Pelias off his throne. And, Jason, unless you will help an old woman at her need, you ought not to be a king. What are kings made for, save to succor the feeble and distressed? But do as you please. Either take me on you back or with my poor old limbs I shall try my best to struggle across the stream."

Saying this, the old woman poked with her staff in the river, as if to find the safest place in its rocky bed where she might make the first step. But Jason, by this time, had grown ashamed of his reluctance to help her. He felt that he could never forgive himself if this poor feeble creature should come to any harm in attempting to wrestle against the headlong current. The good Chiron, whether half horse or no, had taught him that the noblest use of his strength was to assist the weak; and also that he must treat every young woman as if she were his sister, and every old one like a mother. Remembering these maxims, the vigorous and beautiful young man knelt down and requested the good dame to mount upon his back.

"The passage seems to me not very safe," he remarked. "But as your business is so urgent, I will try to carry you across. If the river sweeps you away, it shall take me too."

"That, no doubt, will be a great comfort to both of us," quoth the old woman. "But never fear. We shall get safely across."

She threw her arms around Jason's neck; and lifting her from the ground, he stepped boldly into the raging and foamy current and began to stagger away from the shore. As for the peacock, it alighted on the old dame's shoulder. Jason's two spears, one in each hand, kept him from stumbling and enabled him to feel his way among the hidden rocks; although, every instant, he expected that his companion and himself would go down the stream, together with the driftwood of shattered trees and the carcasses of the sheep and cow. Down came the cold, snowy torrent from the steep side of Olympus, raging and thundering as if it had a real spite against Jason, or, at all events, were determined to snatch off his living burden from his shoulders. When he was halfway across, the uprooted tree (which I have already told you about) broke loose from among the rocks and bore down upon him, with all its splintered branches sticking out like the hundred arms of the giant Briareus. It rushed past, however, without touching him. But the next moment his foot was caught in a crevice between two rocks, and stuck there so fast, that, in the effort to get free, he lost one of his golden-stringed sandals.

At this accident Jason could not help uttering a cry of vexation.

"What is the matter, Jason?" asked the old woman.

"Matter enough," said the young man. "I have lost a sandal here among the rocks. And what sort of figure shall I cut at the court of King Pelias, with a golden-stringed sandal on one foot and the other foot bare!"

"Do not take it to heart," answered his companion, cheerily. "You never met with better fortune than in losing that sandal. It satisfies me that you are the very person whom the Speaking Oak has been talking about."

There was no time, just then, to inquire what the Speaking Oak had said. But the briskness of her tone encouraged the young man; and besides, he had never in his life felt so vigorous and mighty as he was since taking this old woman on his back. Instead of being exhausted, he gathered strength as he went on; and, struggling up against the torrent, he at last gained the opposite shore, clambered up the bank, and set down the old dame and her peacock safely on the grass. As soon as this was done, however, he could not help looking rather despondently at his bare foot, with only a remnant of the golden string of the sandal clinging round his ankle.

"You will get a handsomer pair of sandals by and by," said the old woman, with a kindly look out of her beautiful brown eyes. "Only let King Pelias get a glimpse of that bare foot and you shall see him turn pale as ashes, I promise you. There is your path. Go along, my good Jason, and my blessing go with you. And when you sit on your throne, remember the old woman whom you helped over the river."

With these words, she hobbled away, giving him a smile over her shoulder as she departed. Whether the light of her beautiful brown eyes threw a glory round about her, or whatever the cause might be, Jason fancied that there was something very noble and majestic in her figure, after all, and that, though her gait seemed to be a rheumatic hobble, yet she moved with as much grace and dignity as any queen on earth. Her peacock, which had now fluttered down from her shoulder, strutted behind her in prodigious pomp and spread out its magnificent tail on purpose for Jason to admire it.

When the old dame and her peacock were out of sight, Jason set forward on his journey. After traveling a pretty long distance, he came to a town situated at the foot of a mountain and not a great way from the shore of the sea. On the outside of the town there was an immense crowd of people, not only men and women, but children too, all in their best clothes, and evidently enjoying a holiday. The crowd was thickest toward the seashore; and in that direction, over the people's heads, Jason saw a wreath of smoke curling upward to the blue sky. He inquired of one of the multitude what town it was, near by, and why so many persons were here assembled together.

"This is the kingdom of Iolchos," answered the man, "and we are the subjects of King Pelias. Our monarch has summoned us together that we may see him sacrifice a black bull to Neptune, who, they say, is his Majesty's father. Yonder is the king, where you see the smoke going up from the altar."

While the man spoke, he eyed Jason with great curiosity; for his garb was quite unlike that of the Iolchians, and it looked very odd to see a youth with a leopard's skin over his shoulders and each hand grasping a spear. Jason perceived, too, that the man stared particularly at his feet, one of which, you remember, was bare, while the other was decorated with his father's golden-stringed sandal.

"Look at him! only look at him!" said the man to his next-door neighbor. "Do you see? He wears but one sandal!"

Upon this, first one person and then another began to stare at Jason, and everybody seemed to be greatly struck with something in his aspect; though they turned their eyes much oftener toward his feet than to any other part of his figure. Besides, he could hear them whispering to one another.

"One sandal! One sandal!" they kept saying. "The man with one sandal! Here he is at last!"

Whence has he come? What does he mean to do? What will the king say to the one-sandaled man?"

Poor Jason was greatly abashed, and made up his mind that the people of Iolchos were exceedingly ill-bred to take such public notice of an accidental deficiency in his dress. Meanwhile, whether it was that they hustled him forward, or that Jason, of his own accord, thrust a passage through the crowd, it so happened that he soon found himself close to the smoking altar, where King Pelias was sacrificing the black bull. The murmur and hum of the multitude, in their surprise at the spectacle of Jason with his one bare foot, grew so loud that it disturbed the ceremonies; and the king, holding the great knife with which he was just going to cut the bull's throat, turned angrily about and fixed his eyes on Jason. The people had now withdrawn from around him, so that the youth stood in an open space near the smoking altar, front to front with the angry King Pelias.

"Who are you?" cried the king, with a terrible frown. "And how dare you make this disturbance while I am sacrificing a black bull to my father Neptune?"

"It is no fault of mine," answered Jason. "Your Majesty must blame the rudeness of your subjects, who have raised all this tumult because one of my feet happens to be bare."

When Jason said this, the king gave a quick, startled glance down at his feet.

"Ha!" muttered he, "here is the one-sandaled fellow, sure enough! What can I do with him?"

And he clutched more closely the great knife in his hand, as if he were half a mind to slay Jason instead of the black bull. The people round about caught up the king's words indistinctly as they were uttered; and first there was a murmur among them and then a loud shout.

"The one-sandaled man has come! The prophecy must be fulfilled!"

For you are to know, that, many years before, King Pelias had been told by the Speaking Oak of Dodona that a man with one sandal should cast him down from his throne. On this account, he had given strict orders that nobody should ever come into his presence unless both sandals were securely tied upon his feet; and he kept an officer in his palace, whose sole business it was to examine people's sandals, and to supply them with a new pair, at the expense of the royal treasury, as soon as the old ones began to wear out. In the whole course of the king's reign, he had never been thrown into such a fright and agitation as by the spectacle of poor Jason's bare foot. But, as he was naturally a bold and hard-hearted man, he soon took courage, and began to consider in what way he might rid himself of this terrible one-sandaled stranger.

"My good young man," said King Pelias, taking the softest tone imaginable, in order to throw Jason off his guard, "you are excessively welcome to my kingdom. Judging by your dress, you must have traveled a long distance; for it is not the fashion to wear leopard skins in this part of the world. Pray, what may I call your name? And where did you receive your education?"

"My name is Jason," answered the young stranger. "Ever since my infancy, I have dwelt in the cave of Chiron the Centaur. He was my instructor, and taught me music and horsemanship and how to cure wounds and likewise how to inflict wounds with my weapons!"

"I have heard of Chiron the schoolmaster," replied King Pelias, "and how that there is an immense deal of learning and wisdom in his head, although it happens to be set on a horse's body. It gives be great delight to see one of his scholars at my court. But, to test how much you have profited under so excellent a teacher, will you allow me to ask you a single question?"

"I do not pretend to be very wise," said Jason. "But ask me what you please and I will answer to the best of my ability."

Now King Pelias meant cunningly to entrap the young man and to make him say something that should be the cause of mischief and destruction to himself. So with a crafty and evil smile on his face, he spoke as follows:

"What would you do, brave Jason," asked he, "if there were a man in the world, by whom, as you had reason to believe, you were doomed to be ruined and slain — what would you do, I say, if that man stood before you, and in your power?"

When Jason saw the malice and wickedness which King Pelias could not prevent from gleaming out of his eyes, he probably guessed that the king had discovered what he came for, and that he intended to turn his own words against himself. Still he scorned to tell a falsehood. Like an upright and honorable prince, as he was, he determined to speak out the real truth. Since the king had chosen to ask him the question, and since Jason had promised him an answer, there was no right way save to tell him precisely what would be the most prudent thing to do, if he had his worst enemy in his power. Therefore, after a moment's consideration, he spoke up with a firm and manly voice.

"I would send such a man," said he, "in quest of the Golden Fleece!"

This enterprise, you will understand, was, of all others, the most difficult and dangerous in the world, In the first place, it would be necessary to make a long voyage through unknown seas. There was hardly a hope, or a possibility, that any young man who should undertake this voyage would either succeed in obtaining the Golden Fleece or would survive to return home and tell of the perils he had run. The eyes of King Pelias sparkled with joy, therefore, when he heard Jason's reply.

"Well said, wise man with the one sandal!" cried he. "Go, then, and at the peril of your life bring back the Golden Fleece."

"I go," answered Jason, composedly. "If I fail, you need not fear that I will ever come back to trouble you again. But if I return to Iolchos with the prize, then, King Pelias, you must hasten down from your lofty throne and give me your crown and scepter."

"That I will," said the king, with a sneer. "Meantime, I will keep them very safely for you."

The first thing that Jason thought of doing, after he left the king's presence, was to go to Dodona and inquire of the Speaking Oak what course it was best to pursue. This wonderful tree stood in the center of an ancient wood. Its stately trunk rose a hundred feet into the air, and threw a broad and dense shadow over more than an acre of ground. Standing beneath it, Jason looked up among the knotted branches and green leaves, and into the mysterious heart of the old tree. He spoke aloud, as if he were addressing some person who was hidden in the depths of the foliage.

"What shall I do," said he, "in order to win the Golden Fleece?"

At first there was a deep silence, not only within the shadow of the Speaking Oak, but all through the solitary wood. In a moment or two, however, the leaves of the oak began to stir and rustle, as if a gentle breeze were wandering amongst them, although the other trees of the wood were perfectly still. The sound grew louder and became like the roar of a high wind. By and by, Jason imagined that he could distinguish words, but very confusedly, because each separate leaf of the tree seemed to be a tongue, and the whole myriad of tongues were babbling at once. But the noise waxed broader and deeper, until it resembled a tornado sweeping through the oak and making one great utterance out of the thousand and thousand of little murmurs which each leafy tongue had caused by its rustling. And now, though it still had the tone of mighty wind roaring among the branches, it was also like a deep bass voice, speaking as distinctly as a tree could be expected to speak, the following words:

"Go to Argus, the shipbuilder, and bid him build a galley with fifty oars."

Then the voice melted again into the indistinct murmur of the rustling leaves and died gradually away. When it was quite gone, Jason felt inclined to doubt whether he had actually heard the words, or whether his fancy had not shaped them out of the ordinary sound made by a breeze, while passing through the thick foliage of the tree.

But on inquiry among the people of Iolchos, he found that there was really a man in the city, by the name of Argus, who was a very skilful builder of vessels. This showed some intelligence in the oak; else how should it have known that any such person existed?   At Jason's request, Argus readily consented to build him a galley so big that it sould require fifty strong men to row it; although no vessel of such a size and burden had heretofore been seen in the world. So the head carpenter and all his journeymen and apprentices began their work; and for a good while afterwards, there they were, busily employed, hewing out the timbers, and making a great clatter with their hammers; until the new ship, which was called the "Argo," seemed to quite ready for sea. And, as the Speaking Oak had already given him such good advice, Jason thought that it would not be amiss to ask for a little more. He visited it again, therefore, and standing beside its huge, rough trunk, inquired what he should do next.

This time, there was no such universal quivering of the leaves, throughout the whole tree, as there had been before. But after a while, Jason observed that the foliage of a great branch which stretched above his head had begun to rustle, as if the wind were stirring that one bough, while all the other boughs of the oak were at rest.

"Cut me off!" said the branch, as soon as it could speak distinctly; "cut me off! cut me off! and carve me into a figurehead for your galley."

Accordingly, Jason took the branch at its word and lopped it off the tree. A carver in the neighborhood engaged to make the figurehead. He was a tolerably good workman, and had already carved several figureheads, in what he intended for feminine shapes, and looking pretty much like those which we see nowadays stuck up under a vessel's bowsprit, with great staring eyes, that never wink at the dash of the spray. But (what was very strange) the carver found that his hand was guided by some unseen power and by a skill beyond his own, and that his tools shaped out an image which he had never dreamed of. When the work was finished, it turned out to be the figure of a beautiful woman with a helmet on her head, from beneath which the long ringlets fell down upon her shoulders. On the left arm was a shield, and in its center appeared a lifelike representation of the head of Medusa with the snaky locks. The right arm was extended, as if pointing onward. The face of this wondrous statue, though not angry or forbidding, was so grave and majestic that perhaps you might call it severe; and as for the mouth, it seemed just ready to unclose its lips and utter words of the deepest wisdom.

Jason was delighted with the oaken image, and gave the carver no rest until it was completed and set up where a figurehead had always stood, from that time to this, in the vessel's prow.

"And now," cried he, as he stood gazing at the calm, majestic face of the statue, "I must go to the Speaking Oak, and inquire what next to do."

"There is no need of that, Jason," said a voice which, though it was far lower, reminded him of the mighty tones of the great oak. "When you desire good advice, you can seek it of me."

Jason had been looking straight into the face of the image when these words were spoken. But he could hardly believe either his ears or his eyes. The truth was, however, that the oaken lips had moved, and, to all appearance, the voice had proceeded from the statue's mouth. Recovering a little from his surprise, Jason bethought himself that the image had been carved out of the wood of the Speaking Oak, and that, therefore, it was really no great wonder, but on the contrary, the most natural thing in the world, that it should possess the faculty of speech. It would have been very odd, indeed, if it has not. But certainly it was a great piece of good fortune that he should be able to carry so wise a block of wood along with him in his perilous voyage.

"Tell me, wondrous image," exclaimed Jason, "since you inherit the wisdom of the Speaking Oak of Dodona, whose daughter you are — tell me, where shall I find fifty bold youths who will take each of them an oar of my galley? They must have sturdy arms to row and brave hearts to encounter perils, or we shall never win the Golden Fleece."

"Go," replied the oaken image, "go, summon all the heroes of Greece."

And, in fact, considering what a great deed was to be done, could any advice be wiser than this which Jason received from the figurehead of his vessel: He lost no time in sending messengers to all the cities and making known to the whole people of Greece, that, Prince Jason, the son of King AEson, was going in quest of the Fleece of Gold, and that he desired the help of forty-nine of the bravest and strongest young men alive, to row his vessel and share his dangers. And Jason himself would be the fifieth.

At this news, the adventurous youths all over

the country began to bestir themselves. Some of
them had already fought with giants and slain
dragons; and the younger ones, who had not yet
met with such good fortune, thought it a shame
to have lived so long without getting astride of a
flying serpent or sticking their spears into a
chimera or, at least, thrusting their right arms
down a monstrous lion's throat. There was a fair
prospect that they would meet with plenty of
such adventures before finding the Golden
Fleece. As soon as they could furbish up their
helmets and shields, therefore, and gird on their
trusty swords, they came thronging to Iolchos,
and clambered on board the new galley. Shaking
hands with Jason, they assured him that they did
not care a pin for their lives, but would help row
the vessel to the remotest edge of the world and
as much farther as he might think it best to go.

Many of these brave fellows had been educated
by Chiron, the four-footed pedagogue, and were,
therefore, old schoolmates of Jason, and knew
him to be a lad of spirit. The mighty Hercules,
whose shoulders afterwards held up the sky, was
one of them. And there were Castor and Pollux,
the twin brothers, who were never accused of
being chicken-hearted, although they had been
hatched out of an egg; and Theseus, who was so
renowned for killing the Minotaur; and Lynceus,
with his wonderfully sharp eyes, which could see
through a millstone or look right down into the
depths of the earth and discover the treasures
that were there; and Orpheus, the very best of
harpers, who sang and played upon his lyre so
sweetly that the brute beasts stood upon their
hind legs and capered merrily to the music. Yes,
and at some of his more moving tunes, the rocks

bestirred their moss-grown bulk out of the
ground and a grove of forest trees uprooted
themselves, and, nodding their tops to one
another, preformed a country dance.

One of the rowers was a beautiful young
woman, named Atalanta, who had been nursed
among the mountains by a bear. So light of foot
was this fair damsel that she could step from one
foamy crest of a wave to the foamy crest of
another, without wetting more than the sole of
her sandal. She had grown up in a very wild way,
and talked much about the rights of women, and
loved hunting and war far better than her needle.
But, in my opinion, the most remarkable of this
famous company were two sons of the North
Wind (airy youngsters, and of a rather a
blustering disposition) who had wings on their
shoulders, and, in case of a calm, could puff out
their cheeks and blow almost as fresh a breeze as
their father. I ought not to forget the prophets
and conjurers, of whom there were several in the
crew, and who could foretell what would happen
tomorrow or the next day or a hundred years
hence, but were generally quite unconscious of
what was passing at the moment.

Jason appointed Tiphys to be helmsman,
because he was a stargazer, and knew the points
of the compass. Lynceus, on account of his sharp
sight, was stationed as a lookout in the prow,
where he saw a whole day's sail ahead, but was
rather apt to overlook things that lay directly
under his nose. If the sea only happened to be
deep enough, however, Lynceus could tell you
exactly what kind of rocks or sands were at the
bottom of it; and he often cried out to his
companions that they were sailing over heaps of

sunken treasure, which yet he was none the richer for beholding. To confess the truth, few people believed him when he said it.

Well! But when the Argonauts, as these fifty brave adventurers were called, had prepared everything for the voyage, an unforeseen difficulty threatened to end it before it was begun. The vessel, you must understand, was so long and broad and ponderous, that the united force of all the fifty was insufficient to shove her into the water. Hercules, I suppose, had not grown to his full strength, else he might have set her afloat as easily as a little boy launches his boat upon a puddle. But here were these fifty heroes, pushing and straining and growing red in the face, without making the "Argo" start an inch. At last, quite wearied out, they sat themselves down on the shore, exceedingly disconsolate, and thinking that the vessel must be left to rot and fall in pieces, and that they must either swim across the ssea or lose the Golden Fleece.

All at once, Jason bethought himself of the galley's miraculous figurehead.

"O daughter of the Speaking Oak," cried he, "how shall we set to work to get our vessel into the water?"

"Seat yourselves," answered the image (for it had known what ought to be done from the very first, and was only waiting for the question to be put) — "seat yourselves and handle your oars, and let Orpheus play upon his harp."

Immediately the fifty heroes got on board and seizing their oars, held them perpendicularly in the air, while Orpheus (who liked such a task far better than rowing) swept his fingers across the harp. At the first ringing note of the music, they felt the vessel stir. Orpheus thrummed away briskly and the galley slid at once into the sea, dipping her prow so deeply that the figurehead drank the wave with its marvelous lips and rose again as buoyant as a swan. The rowers plied their fifty oars; the white foam boiled up before the prow; the water gurgled and bubbled in their wake; while Orpheus continued to play so lively a strain of music that the vessel seemed to dance over the billows by way of keeping time to it. Thus triumphantly did the "Argo" sail out of the harbor, amidst the huzzas and good wishes of everybody except the wicked old Pelias, who stood on a promontory, scowling at her, and wishing that he could blow out of his lungs the tempest of wrath that was in his heart and so sink the galley will all on board. When they had sailed above fifty miles over the sea, Lynceus happened to cast his sharp eyes behind, and said that there was this bad-hearted king, still perched upon the promontory and scowling so gloomily that it looked like a black thundercloud in that quarter of the horizon.

In order to make the time pass away more pleasantly during the voyage, the heroes talked about the Golden Fleece. It originally belonged, it appears, to a Bœotian ram, who had taken on his back two children, when in danger of their lives, and fled with them over land and sea, as far as Colchis. One of the children, whose name was Helle, fell into the sea and was drowned. But the other (a little boy, named Phrixus) was brought safe ashore by the faithful ram, who, however, was so exhausted that he immediately lay down and died. In memory of this good deed, and as a token of his true heart, the fleece of the poor dead ram was miraculously changed to gold, and became one of the most beautiful objects ever seen on earth. It was hung upon a tree in a sacred grove, where it had now been kept I know not how many years, and was the envy of mighty kings, who had nothing so magnificent in any of their palaces.

If I were to tell you all the adventures of the Argonauts, it would take me till nightfall and perhaps a great deal longer. There was no lack of wonderful events, as you may judge from what you have already heard. At a certain island they were hospitably received by King Cyzicus, its sovereign, who made a feast for them, and treated them like brothers. But the Argonauts saw that this good king looked downcast and very much troubled, and they therefore inquired of him what was the matter. King Cyzicus hereupon informed them that he and his subjects were greatly abused and incommoded by the inhabitants of a neighboring mountain, who made war upon them and killed many people and ravaged the country. And while they were talking about it, Cyzicus pointed to the mountain and asked Jason and his companions what they saw there.

"I see some very tall objects," answered Jason; "but they are at such a distance that I cannot distinctly make out what they are. To tell your Majesty the truth, they look so very strangely that I am inclined to think them clouds, which have chanced to take something like human shapes."

"I see them very plainly," remarked Lynceus, whose eyes, you know, were as farsighted as a telescope. "They are a band of enormous giants, all of whom have six arms apiece, and a club, a sword, or some other weapon in each of their hands."

"You have excellent eyes," said King Cyzicus. "Yes; they are six-armed giants, as you say, and these are the enemies whom I and my subjects have to contend with."

The next day, when the Argonauts were about setting sail, down came these terrible giants, stepping a hundred yards at a stride, brandishing their arms apiece and looking very formidable, so far aloft in the air. Each of these monsters was able to carry on a whole war by himself; for with one of his arms he could fling immense stones and wield a club with another and a sword with a third, while a fourth was poking a long spear at the enemy, and the fifth and sixth were shooting him with a bow and arrow. But, luckily, though the giants were so huge and had so many arms, they had each but one heart, and that no bigger nor braver than the heart of an ordinary man. Besides, if they had been like the hundred-armed Briareus, the brave Argonauts would have given them their hands full of fight. Jason and his friends went boldly to meet them, slew a great many, and made the rest take to their heels, so that if the giants had had six legs apiece instead of six arms, it would have served them better to run away with.

Another strange adventure happened when the voyagers came to Thrace, where they found a poor blind king, named Phineus, deserted by his subjects and living in a very sorrowful way, all by himself. On Jason's inquiring whether they could do him any service, the king answered that he

was terribly tormented by three great winged
creatures, called Harpies, which had the faces of
women, and the wings, bodies, and claws of
vultures. These ugly wretches were in the habit
of snatching away his dinner and allowed him no
peace of his life. Upon hearing this, the
Argonauts spread a plentiful feast on the seashore, well knowing, from what the blind king
said of their greediness, that the Harpies would
snuff up the scent of the victuals and quickly
come to steal them away. And so it turned out;
for, hardly was the table set before the three
hideous vulture women came flapping their
wings, seized the food in their talons, and flew
off as fast as they could. But the two sons of the
North Wind drew their swords, spread their
pinions, and set off through the air in pursuit of
the thieves, whom they at last overtook among
some islands, after a chase of hundreds of miles.
The two winged youths blustered terribly at the
Harpies (for they had the rough temper of their
father), and so frightened them with their drawn
swords that they solemnly promised never to
trouble King Phineus again.

Then the Argonauts sailed onward and met
with many other marvelous incidents, any one of
which would make a story by itself. At one time
they landed on an island and were reposing on the
grass, when they suddenly found themselves
assailed by what seemed a shower of steel-
headed arrows. Some of them stuck in the
ground, while others hit against their shields and
several penetrated their flesh. The fifty heroes
started up and looked about them for the hidden
enemy, but could fine none, nor see any spot, on
the whole island, where even a single archer

could lie concealed. Still, however, the steel-headed arrows came whizzing among them; and, at last, happening to look upward, they beheld a large flock of birds, hovering and wheeling aloft and shooting their feathers down upon the Argonauts. These feathers were the steel-headed arrows that had so tormented them. There was no possibility of making any resistance; and the fifty heroic Argonauts might all have been killed or wounded by a flock of troublesome birds, without ever setting eyes on the Golden Fleece, if Jason had not thought of asking the advice of the oaken image.

So he ran to the galley as fast as his legs would carry him.

"O daughter of the Speaking Oak," cried he, all out of breath, "we need your wisdom more than ever before! We are in great peril from a flock of birds, who are shooting us with their steel-pointed feathers. What can we do to drive them away?"

"Make a clatter on your shields," said the image.

On receiving this excellent counsel, Jason hurried back to his companions (who were far more dismayed than when they fought with the six-armed giants) and bade them strike with their swords upon their brazen shields. Forthwith the fifty heroes set heartily to work, banging with might and main, and raised such a terrible clatter that the birds made what haste they could to get away; and though they had shot half the feathers out of their wings, they were soon seen skimming among the clouds, a long distance off, and looking like a flock of wild geese. Orpheus celebrated this victory by playing a triumphant anthem on his harp, and sang so melodiously that Jason begged him to desist, lest, as the steel-feathered birds had been driven away by an ugly sound, they might be enticed back again by a sweet one.

While the Argonauts remained on this island, they saw a small vessel approaching the shore, in which were two young men of princely demeanor and exceedingly handsome as young princes generally were in those days. Now, who do you imagine these two voyagers turned out to be? Why, if you will believe me, they were the sons of that very Phrixus, who, in his childhood, had been carried to Colchis on the back of the golden-fleeced ram. Since that time, Phrixus had married the king's daughter; and the two young princes had been born and brought up at Colchis and had spent their play days in the outskirts of the grove, in the center of which the Golden Fleece was hanging upon a tree. They were now on their way to Greece, in hopes of getting back a kingdom that had been wrongully taken from their father.

When the princes understood whither the Argonauts were going, they offered to turn back and guide them to Colchis. At the same time, however, they spoke as if it were very doubtful whether Jason would succeed in getting the Golden Fleece. According to their account, the tree on which it hung was guarded by a terrible dragon, who never failed to devour, at one mouthful, every person who might venture within his reach.

"There are other difficulties in the way," continued the young princes. "But is not this enough? Ah, brave Jason, turn back before it is

too late. It would grieve us to the heart if you
and your nine and forty brave companions should
be eaten up, at fifty mouthfuls, by this execrable
dragon."

"My young friends," quietly replied Jason, "I do
not wonder that you think the dragon very
terrible. You have grown up from infancy in the
fear of this monster, and therefore still regard
him with the awe that children feel for the
bugbears and hobgoblins which their nurses have
talked to them about. But, in my view of the
matter, the dragon is merely a pretty large
serpent, who is not half so likely to snap me up
at one mouthful as I am to cut off his ugly head
and strip the skin from his body. At all events,
turn back who may, I will never see Greece again
unless I carry with me the Golden Fleece."

"We will none of us turn back!" cried his nine
and forty brave comrades. "Let us get on board
the galley this instant; and if the dragon is to
make a breakfast of us, much good may it do
him."

And Orpheus (whose custom it was to set
everything to music) began to harp and sing most
gloriously, and made every mother's son of them
feel as if nothing in this world were so delectable
as to fight dragons, and nothing so truly honorable as to be eaten up at one mouthful, in case of
the worst.

After this (being now under the guidance of
the two princes, who were well acquainted with
the way) they quickly sailed to Colchis. When
the king of the country, whose name was AEetes,
heard of their arrival, he instantly summoned
Jason to court. The king was a stern and cruel-
looking potentate; and though he put on as polite

and hospitable an expression as he could, Jason did not like his face a whit better than that of the wicked King Pelias, who dethroned his father.

"You are welcome, brave Jason," said King AEetes. "Pray, are you on a pleasure voyage? Or do you meditate the discovery of unknown islands? Or what other cause has procured me the happiness of seeing you at my court?"

"Great sir," replied Jason, with an obeisance — for Chiron had taught him how to behave with propriety, whether to kings or beggars — "I have come hither with a purpose which I now beg your Majesty's permission to execute. King Pelias, who sits on my father's throne (to which he has no more right than to the one on which your excellent Majesty is now seated), has engaged to come down from it, and to give me his crown and scepter, provided I bring him the Golden Fleece. This, as your Majesty is aware, is now hanging on a tree here at Colchis; and I humbly solicit your gracious leave to take it away."

In spite of himself, the king's face twisted itself into an angry frown; for, above all things else in the world, he prized the Golden Fleece, and was even suspected of having done a very wicked act in order to get it into his own possession. It put him into the worst possible humor, therefore, to hear that the gallant Prince Jason and forty-nine of the bravest young warriors of Greece had come to Colchis with the sole purpose of taking away his chief treasure.

"Do you know," asked King AEetes, eying Jason very sternly, "what are the conditions which you must fulfil before getting possession of the Golden Fleece?"

"I have heard," rejoined the youth, "that a dragon lies beneath the tree on which the prize hangs, and that whoever approaches him runs the risk of being devoured at a mouthful."

"True," said the king, with a smile that did not look particularly good-natured. "Very true, young man. But there are other things as hard, or perhaps a little harder, to be done, before you can even have the privilege of being devoured by the dragon. For example, you must first tame my two brazen-footed and brazen-lunged bulls, which Vulcan, the wonderful blacksmith, made for me. There is a furnace in each of their stomachs; and they breathe such hot fire out of their mouths and nostrils that nobody has hither-to gone nigh them without being instantly burned to a small, black cinder. What do you think of this, my brave Jason?"

"I must encounter the peril," answered Jason, composedly, "since it stands in the way of my purpose."

After taming the fiery bulls," continued King AEetes, who was determined to scare Jason if possible, "you must yoke them to a plow, and must plow the sacred earth in the grove of Mars, and sow some of the same dragon's teeth from which Cadmus raised a crop of armed men. They are an unruly set of reprobates, those sons of the dragon's teeth; and unless you treat them suitab-ly, they will fall upon you sword in hand. You and your nine and forty Argonauts, my bold Jason, are hardly numerous or strong enough to fight with such a host as will spring up."

"My master, Chiron," replied Jason, "taught me, long ago, the story of Cadmus. Perhaps I can manage the quarrelsome sons of the dragon's teeth as well as Cadmus did."

"I wish the dragon had him," muttered King
AEetes to himself, "and the four-footed pedant,
his schoolmaster, into the bargain. Why, what a
foolhardy, self-conceited coxcomb he is! We'll
see what my fire-breathing bulls will do for him.
Well, Prince Jason," he continued, aloud, and as
complaisantly as he could, "make yourself
comfortable for today, and tomorrow morning,
since you insist upon it, you shall try your skill at
the plow."

While the king talked with Jason, a beautiful
young woman was standing behind the throne.
She fixed her eyes earnestly upon the youthful
stranger and listened attentively to every word
that was spoken; and when Jason withdrew from
the king's presence, this young woman followed
him out of the room.

"I am the king's daughter," she said to him,
"and my name is Medea. I know a great deal of
which other young princesses are ignorant, and
can do many things which they would be afraid so
much as to dream of. If you will trust to me, I
can instruct you how to tame the fiery bulls and
sow the dragon's teeth and get the Golden
Fleece."

"Indeed, beautiful princess," answered Jason,
"if you will do me this service, I promise to be
grateful to you my whole life long."

Gazing at Medea, he beheld a wonderful
intelligence in her face. She was one of those
persons whose eyes are full of mystery; so that
while looking into them, you seem to see a very
great way, as into a deep well, yet can never be
certain whether you see into the farthest depths
or whether there be not something else hidden at

the bottom. If Jason had been capable of fearing anything, he would have been afraid of making this young princess his enemy; for, beautiful as she now looked, she might, the very next instant, become as terrible as the dragon that kept watch over the Golden Fleece.

"Princess," he exclaimed, "you seem indeed very wise and very powerful. But how can you help me to do the things of which you speak? Are you an enchantress?"

"Yes, Prince Jason," answered Medea, with a smile, "you have hit upon the truth. I am an enchantress. Circe, my father's sister, taught me to be one, and I could tell you, if I pleased, who was the old woman with the peacock, the pomegranate, and the cuckoo staff, whom you carried over the river; and, likewise, who it is that speaks through the lips of the oaken image, that stands in the prow of your galley. I am acquainted with some of your secrets, you perceive. It is well for you that I am favorably inclined; for, otherwise, you would hardly escape being snapped up by the dragon."

"I should not so much care for the dragon," replied Jason, "if I only knew how to manage the brazen-footed and fiery-lunged bulls."

"If you are as brave as I think you, and as you have need to be," said Medea, "your own bold heart will teach you that there is but one way of dealing with a mad bull. What it is I leave you to find out in the moment of peril. As for the fiery breath of these animals, I have a charmed ointment here which will prevent you from being burned up, and cure you if you chance to be a little scorched."

So she put a golden box into his hand and

directed him how to apply the perfumed unguent which it contained, and where to meet her at midnight.

"Only be brave," added she, "and before daybreak the brazen bulls shall be tamed."

The young man assured her that his heart would not fail him. He then rejoined his comrades, and told them what had passed between the princess and himself, and warned them to be in readiness in case there might be need of their help.

At the appointed hour he met the beautiful Medea on the marble steps of the king's palace. She gave him a basket, in which were the dragon's teeth, just as they had been pulled out of the monster's jaws by Cadmus long ago. Medea then led Jason down the palace steps, and through the silent streets of the city, and into the royal pasture ground, where the two brazen-footed bulls were kept. It was a starry night, with a bright gleam along the eastern edge of the sky, where the moon was soon going to show herself. After entering the pasture, the princess paused and looked around.

"There they are," said she, "reposing themselves and chewing their fiery cuds in that farthest corner of the field. It will be excellent sport, I assure you, when they catch a glimpse of your figure. My father and all his court delight in nothing so much as to see a stranger trying to yoke them, in order to come at the Golden Fleece. It makes a holiday in Colchis whenever such a thing happens. For my part, I enjoy it immensely. You cannot imagine in what a mere twinkling of an eye their hot breath shrivels a young man into a black cinder."

"Are you sure, beautiful Medea," asked Jason, "quite sure, that the unguent in the gold box will prove a remedy against those terrible burns?"

"If you doubt, if you are in the least afraid," said the princess, looking him in the face by the dim starlight, "you had better never have been born than go a step nigher to the bulls."

But Jason had set his heart steadfastly on getting the Golden Fleece; and I positively doubt whether he would have gone back without it, even had he been certain of finding himself turned into a red-hot cinder or a handful of white ashes, the instant he made a step farther. He therefore let go Medea's hand and walked boldly forward in the direction whither she had pointed. At some distance before him he perceived four streams of fiery vapor, regularly appearing and again vanishing, after dimly lighting up the surrounding obscurity. These, you will understand, were caused by the breath of the brazen bulls, which was quietly stealing out of their four nostrils, as they lay chewing their cuds.

At the first two or three steps which Jason made, the four fiery streams appeared to gush out somewhat more plentifully; for the two brazen bulls had heard his foot tramp and were lifting up their hot noses to snuff the air. He went a little farther, and by the way in which the red vapor now spouted fourth, he judged that the creatures had got upon their feet. Now he could see glowing sparks and vivid jets of flame. At the next step, each of the bulls made the pasture echo with a terrible roar, while the burning breath, which they thus belched forth, lit up the whole field with a momentary flash. One other stride did bold Jason make; and, suddenly, as a streak of lightning, on came these fiery animals, roaring like thunder, and sending out sheets of white flame, which so kindled up the scene that the young man could discern every object more distinctly than by daylight. Most distinctly of all he saw the two horrible creatures galloping right down upon him, their brazen hoofs rattling and ringing over the ground and their tails sticking up stiffly into the air, as has always been the fashion with angry bulls. Their breath scorched the herbage before them. So intensely hot was it, indeed, that it caught a dry tree, under which Jason was now standing, and set it all in a light blaze. But as for Jason himself (thanks to Medea's enchanted ointment), the white flame curled around his body, without injuring him a lot more than if he had been made of asbestos.

Greatly encouraged at finding himself not yet turned into a cinder, the young man awaited the attack of the bulls. Just as the brazen brutes fancied themselves sure of tossing him into the air, he caught one of them by the horn and the other by his screwed-up tail, and held them in a grip like that of an iron vise, one with his right hand, the other with his left. Well, he must have been wonderfully strong in his arms, to be sure. But the secret of the matter was that the brazen bulls were enchanted creatures, and that Jason had broken the spell of their fiery fierceness by his bold way of handling them. And, ever since that time, it has been the favorite method of brave men, when danger assails them, to do what they call, "taking the bull by the horns"; and to grip him by the tail is pretty much the same thing — that is, to throw aside fear and overcome the peril by despising it.

It was now easy to yoke the bulls and to harness them to the plow, which had lain rusting on the ground for a great many years gone by; so long was it before anybody could be found capable of plowing that piece of land. Jason, I suppose, had been taught how to draw a furrow by the good old Chiron, who, perhaps, used to allow himself to be harnessed to the plow. At any rate, our hero succeeded perfectly well in breaking up the greensward; and, by the time that the moon was a quarter of her journey up the sky, the plowed field lay before him, a large tract of black earth, ready to be sown with the dragon's teeth. So Jason scattered them broadcast and harrowed them into the soil with a brush harrow, and took his stand on the edge of the field, anxious to see what would happen next.

"Must we wait long for harvest time?" he inquired of Medea, who was now standing by his side.

"Whether sooner or later, it will be sure to come," answered the princess. "A crop of armed men never fails to spring up, when the dragon's teeth have been sown."

The moon was now high aloft in the heavens and threw its bright beams over the plowed field, where as yet there was nothing to be seen. Any farmer, on viewing it, would have said that Jason must wait weeks before the green blades would peep from among the clods, and whole months before the yellow grain would be ripened for the sickle. But by and by, all over the field, there was something that glistened in the moonbeams, like sparkling drops of dew. These bright objects sprouted higher and proved to be the steel heads of spears. Then there was a dazzling gleam from

a vast number of polished brass helmets, beneath
which, as they grew father out of the soil,
appeared the dark and bearded visages of
warriors, struggling to free themselves from the
imprisoning earth. The first look that they gave
at the upper world was a glare of wrath and
defiance. Next were seen their bright breastplates; in every right hand there was a sword or a
spear, and on each left arm a shield; and when
this strange crop of warriors had but half grown
out of the earth, they struggled — such was their
impatience of restraint — and, as it were, tore
themselves up by the roots. Wherever a dragon's
tooth had fallen, there stood a man armed for
battle. They made a clangor with their swords
against their shields and eyed one another
fiercely; for they had come into this beautiful
world and into the peaceful moonlight, full of
rage and stormy passions, and ready to take the
life of every human brother, in recompense of
the boon of their own existence.

There have been many other armies in the
world that seemed to possess the same fierce
nature with the one which had now sprouted from
the dragon's teeth; but these, in the moonlit
field, were the more excusable, because they
never had women for their mothers. And how it
would have rejoiced any great captain, who was
bent on conquering the world, like Alexander or
Napoleon, to raise a crop of armed soldiers as
easily as Jason did!

For a while, the warriors stood flourishing
their weapons, clashing their swords against their
shields, and boiling over with the red-hot thirst
for battle. Then they began to shout: "Show us
the enemy! Lead us to the charge! Death or

victory! Come on, brave comrades! Conquer or
die!" and a hundred other outcries, such as men
always bellow forth on a battle field, and which
these dragon people seemed to have at their
tongues' ends. At last, the front rank caught
sight of Jason, who, beholding the flash of so
many weapons in the moonlight, has thought it
best to draw his sword. In a moment all the sons
of the dragon's teeth appeared to take Jason for
an enemy; and crying with one voice, "Guard the
Golden Fleece!" they ran at him with uplifted
swords and protruded spears. Jason knew that it
would be impossible to withstand this bloodthirsty battalion with his single arm, but determined, since there was nothing better to be done,
to die as valiantly as if he himself had sprung
from a dragon's tooth.

Medea, however, bade him snatch up a stone
from the ground.

"Throw it among them quickly!" cried she. "It
is the only way to save yourself."

The armed men were now so nigh that Jason
could discern the fire flashing out of their
enraged eyes, when he let fly the stone, and saw
it strike the helmet of a tall warrior, who was
rushing upon him with his blade aloft. The stone
glanced from this man's helmet to the shield of
his nearest comrade, and thence flew right into
the angry face of another, hitting him smartly
between the eyes. Each of the three who had
been struck by the stone took it for granted that
his next neighbor had given him a blow; and
instead of running any farther toward Jason, they
began a fight among themselves. The confusion
spread through the host, so that it seemed
scarcely a moment before they were all hacking,

hewing, and stabbing at one another, lopping off
arms, heads, and legs, and doing such memorable
deeds that Jason was filled with immense admiration; although, at the same time, he could not
help laughing to behold these mighty men
punishing each other for an offense which he
himself had committed. In an incredibly short
space of time (almost as short, indeed, as it had
taken them to grow up) all but one of the heroes
of the dragon's teeth were stretched lifeless on
the field. The last survivor, the bravest and
strongest of the whole, had just force enough to
wave his crimson sword over his head, and give a
shout of exultation, crying, "Victory! Victory!
Immortal fame!" when he himself fell down and
lay quietly among his slain brethren.

And there was the end of the army that had
sprouted from the dragon's teeth. That fierce
and feverish fight was the only enjoyment which
they had tasted on this beautiful earth.

"Let them sleep in the bed of honor," said the
Princess Medea, with a sly smile at Jason. "The
world will always have simpletons enough, just
like them, fighting and dying for they know not
what, and fancying that posterity will take the
trouble to put laurel wreaths on their rusty and
battered helmets. Could you help smiling, Prince
Jason, to see the self-conceit of that last fellow,
just as he tumbled down?"

"It made me very sad," answered Jason, grave-
ly. "And to tell you the truth, princess, the
Golden Fleece does not appear so well worth the
winning, after what I have here beheld."

"You will think differently in the morning,"
said Medea. "True, the Golden Fleece may not
be so valuable as you have thought it; but then

there is nothing better in the world; and one must needs have an object, you know. Come! Your night's work has been well performed; and tomorrow you can inform King Æetes that the first part of your allotted task is fulfilled."

Agreeably to Medea's advice, Jason went betimes in the morning to the palace of King Æestes. Entering the presence-chamber, he stood at the foot of the throne and made a low obeisance.

"Your eyes look heavy, Prince Jason," observed the king; "you appear to have spent a sleepless night. I hope you have been considering the matter a little more wisely and have concluded not to get yourself scorched to a cinder, in attempting to tame my brazen-lunged bulls."

"That is already accomplished, may it please your Majesty," replied Jason. "The bulls have been tamed and yoked; the field has been plowed; the dragon's teeth have been sown broadcast and harrowed into the soil; the crop of armed warriors has sprung up and they have slain one another to the last man. And now I solicit your Majesty's permission to encounter the dragon, that I may take down the Golden Fleece from the tree and depart with my nine and forty comrades."

King Æetes scowled, and looked very angry and excessively disturbed; for he knew that, in accordance with his kingly promise, he ought now to permit Jason to win the fleece, if his courage and skill should enable him to do so. But since the young man had met with such good luck in the matter of the brazen bulls and the dragon's teeth, the king feared that he would be equally successful in slaying the dragon. And therefore, though he would gladly have seen Jason snapped up at a mouthful, he was resolved (and it was a very wrong thing of this wicked potentate) not to run any further risk of losing his beloved fleece.

"You never would have succeeded in this business, young man," said he, "if my undutiful daughter Medea had not helped you with her enchantments. Had you acted fairly, you would have been, at this instant, a black cinder, or a handful of white ashes. I forbid you, on pain of death, to make any more attempts to get the Golden Fleece. To speak my mind plainly, you shall never set eyes on so much as one of its glistening locks."

Jason left the king's presence in great sorrow and anger. He could think of nothing better to be done than to summon together his forty-nine brave Argonauts, march at once to the grove of Mars, slay the dragon, take possession of the Golden Fleece, get on board the "Argo," and spread all sail for Iolchos. The success of this scheme depended, it is true, on the doubtful point whether all the fifty heroes might not be snapped up, at so many mouthfuls, by the dragon. But, as Jason was hastening down the palace steps, the Princess Medea called after him and beckoned him to return. Her black eyes shone upon him with such a keen intelligence that he felt as if there were a serpent peeping out of them; and although she had done him so much service only the night before, he was by no means very certain that she would not do him an equally great mischief before sunset. These enchantresses, you must know, are never to be depended upon.

"What says King Æetes, my royal and unright

father?" inquired Medea, slightly smiling. "Will he give you the Golden Fleece without any further risk or trouble?"

"On the contrary," answered Jason, "he is very angry with me for taming the brazen bulls and sowing the dragon's teeth. And he forbids me to make any more attempts and positively refuses to give up the Golden Fleece, whether I slay the dragon or no."

"Yes, Jason," said the princess, "and I can tell you more. Unless you set sail from Colchis before tomorrow's sunrise, the king means to burn your fifty-oared galley and put yourself and your forty-nine brave comrades to the sword. But be of good courage. The Golden Fleece you shall have, if it lies within the power of my enchantments to get it for you. Wait for me here an hour before midnight."

At the appointed hour, you might again have seen Prince Jason and the Princess Medea, side by side, stealing through the streets of Colchis, on their way to the sacred grove, in the center of which the Golden Fleece was suspended from a tree. While they were crossing the pasture ground, the brazen bulls came toward Jason, lowing, nodding their heads, and thrusting forth their snouts, which, as other cattle do, they loved to have rubbed and caressed by a friendly hand. Their fierce nature was thoroughly tamed; and, with their fierceness, the two furnaces in their stomachs had likewise been extinguished, insomuch that they probably enjoyed far more comfort in gazing and chewing their cuds than ever before. Indeed, it had heretofore been a great inconvenience to these poor animals, that, whenever they wished to eat a mouthful of grass,

the fire out of their nostrils had shriveled it up
before they could manage to crop it. How they
contrived to keep themselves alive is more than I
can imagine. But now, instead of emitting jets
of flame and streams of sulphureous vapor, they
breathed the very sweetest of cow breath.

After kindly patting the bulls, Jason followed
Medea's guidance into the grove of Mars, where
the great oak trees that had been growing for
centuries, threw so thick a shade that the
moonbeams struggled vainly to find their way
through it. Only here and there a glimmer fell
upon the leaf-strewn earth, or now and then a
breeze stirred the boughs aside and gave Jason a
glimpse of the sky, lest, in that deep obscurity,
he might forget that there was one overhead. At
length, when they had gone farther and farther
into the heart of the duskiness, Medea squeezed
Jason's hand.

"Look yonder," she whispered. "Do you see
it?"

Gleaming among the venerable oaks there was
a radiance, not like the moonbeams, but rather
resembling the golden glory of the setting sun. It
proceeded from an object which appeared to be
suspended at about a man's height from the
ground, a little farther within the wood.

"What is it?" asked Jason.

"Have you come so far to seek it," exclaimed
Medea, "and do you not recognize the meed of all
your toils and perils, when it glitters before your
eyes? It is the Golden Fleece."

Jason went onward a few steps farther and
then stopped to gaze. Oh, how beautiful it
looked, shining with a marvelous light of its own,
that inestimable prize which so many heroes had

longed to behold, but had perished in the quest of it, either by the perils of their voyage, or by the fiery breath of the brazen-lunged bulls.

"How gloriously it shines!" cried Jason, in a rapture. "It has surely been dipped in the richest gold of sunset. Let me hasten onward and take it to my bosom."

"Stay," said Medea, holding him back. "Have you forgotten what guards it?"

To say the truth, in the joy of beholding the object of his desires, the terrible dragon had quite slipped out of Jason's memory. Soon, however, something came to pass that reminded him what perils were still to be encountered. An antelope, that probably mistook the yellow radiance for sunrise, came bounding fleetly through the grove. He was rushing straight toward the Golden Fleece, when suddenly there was a frightful hiss, and the immense head and half the scaly body of the dragon was thrust forth (for he was twisted round the trunk of the tree on which the fleece hung), and, seizing the poor antelope, swallowed him with one snap of his jaws.

After this feat, the dragon seemed sensible that some other living creature was within reach, on which he felt inclined to finish his meal. In various directions he kept poking his ugly snout among the trees, stretching out his neck a terrible long way, now here, now there, and now close to the spot where Jason and the princess were hiding behind an oak. Upon my word, as the head came waving and undulating through the air and reaching almost within arm's length of Prince Jason, it was a very hideous and uncomfortable sight. The gape of his enormous jaws was nearly as wide as the gateway of the king's palace.

"Well, Jason," whispered Medea (for she was ill-natured, as all enchantresses are, and wanted to make the bold youth tremble), "what do you think now of your prospect of winning the Golden Fleece?"

Jason answered only by drawing his sword and making a step forward.

"Stay, foolish youth," said Medea, grasping his arm. "Do not you see that you are lost without me as your good angel? In this gold box I have a magic potion, which will do the dragon's business far more effectually than your sword."

The dragon had probably heard the voices; for, swift as lightning, his black head and forked tongue came hissing among the trees again, darting full forty feet at a stretch. As it approached, Medea tossed the contents of the gold box right down the monster's wide open throat. Immediately, with an outrageous hiss and a tremendous wriggle — flinging his tail up to the tiptop of the tallest tree, and shattering all its branches as it crashed heavily down again — the dragon fell at full length upon the ground, and lay quite motionless.

"It is only a sleeping potion," said the enchantress to Prince Jason. "One always finds a use for these mischievous creatures, sooner or later; so I did not wish to kill him outright. Quick! Snatch the prize and let us begone. You have won the Golden Fleece."

Jason caught the fleece from the tree and hurried through the grove, the deep shadows of which were illuminated as he passed by the golden glory of the precious object that he bore along. A little way before him, he beheld the old woman whom he had helped over the stream, with her peacock beside her. She clapped her hands for joy, and beckoning him to make haste, disappeared among the duskiness of the trees. Espying the two winged sons of the North Wind (who were disporting themselves in the moon-light, a few hundred feet aloft), Jason bade them tell the rest of the Argonauts to embark as speedily as possible. But Lynceus, with his sharp eyes, had already caught a glimpse of him, bringing the Golden Fleece, although several stone walls, a hill, and the black shadows of the grove of Mars intervened between. By his advice, the heroes had seated themselves on the benches of the galley, with their oars held perpendicularly, ready to let fall into the water.

As Jason drew near, he heard the Talking Image calling to him with more than ordinary eagerness, in its grave, sweet voice:

"Make haste, Prince Jason! For your life, make haste!"

With one bound he leaped aboard. At sight of the glorious radiance of the Golden Fleece, the nine and forty heroes gave a mighty shout, and Orpheus, striking his harp, sang a song of triumph, to the cadence of which the galley flew over the water, homeward bound, as if careering along with wings!